S0-CFK-131

Talk Me Into It

Talk Me Into It

Preparing Children
for School Success
Through Language

A Guide for Parents, Caregivers, and
Early Childhood Educators

Susan L. Pike, Ph.D.
Speech-language Pathologist

401.9
PL36

Copyright © 2005 by Susan L. Pike, Ph.D.

Cover Photos: Comstock Images / Getty Images
Chapter introductory quotes: Klein, Allen. *Winning Words*. New York: Portland House, 2002.

Library of Congress Control Number: 2005906127
ISBN :   Hardcover   1-4134-9215-0
                Softcover   1-4134-9214-2

All rights reserved. The enclosed material has been copyrighted by the author. Duplication of any of its contents without the author's permission will constitute a violation of copyright law.

This book was printed in the United States of America.

The material presented in this book is available in live workshops that include videotape presentations and hands-on activities. Information about future workshops will be posted on the Web site listed below. In-service workshops are available to organizations and may be arranged by contacting the author.

Susan L. Pike, Ph.D.
1-914-242-5476
E-mail: Info@SusanPike.com
www.SusanPike.com

To order additional copies of this book, contact:
Xlibris Corporation
1-888-795-4274
www.Xlibris.com
Orders@Xlibris.com
27417

Contents

Foreword

I am blessed to spend my days interacting with three- and four-year-old children, most of whom are coming to see me so that they can learn to "talk better." In the course of working with these preschoolers and their parents, I have found a large gap between the professional knowledge base that is part of every speech-language pathologist's routine training and what the typical parent knows. Parents are generally eager to promote their child's development but have neither the time nor the wherewithal to read professional textbooks on this subject. Yet whether they realize it or not, parents and caregivers are affecting children's communication development on a daily basis. They can make an enormous contribution to a child's success simply by becoming more aware of how everyday interactions affect language acquisition. During this period of development, there is a wide range of what is considered normal. Some parents who compare their children to others of the same age become anxious or confused. Pediatricians who used to dismiss nearly all cases of late talking by saying "Don't worry, she'll grow out of it" are now much more aware of the benefits of early intervention. Yet even if there is no diagnosable problem, many parents look in vain for good information in this area. *Talk Me Into It* is the culmination of a lifelong vocation in learning about, and working with, young children. I believe that parents, day-care providers, and preschool teachers will find this a user-friendly book, with little jargon, a book that will inform and assist them in making the most of their interaction with young children.

About the Author

Dr. Susan Pike is a pediatric speech-language pathologist with certification from the American Speech-Language-Hearing Association. She has worked with hundreds of children in both public and private schools, as well as in clinical settings, and has designed and taught a special education classroom program for young children with language and learning difficulties. With over twenty years of experience in diagnosing and treating a variety of speech and language disorders, she brings a lifelong accumulation of knowledge and expertise to share with her readers. She holds a master's degree in speech-language pathology from Columbia University and a Ph.D. from the University of Virginia, where she taught courses in preschool and school-age language problems and conducted research in parent-child interaction. She has been a presenter at state and national conventions and has conducted workshops and training for day-care and preschool personnel. She currently manages a private practice in northern Westchester County, New York.

Introduction

Why Every Parent Should Read This Book

The following are some statistics:

- In a survey of seven thousand kindergarten teachers (part of a study conducted by the Carnegie Foundation for the Advancement of Teaching in the 1980s), the teachers were asked what problem *most* restricted school readiness. The majority responded, "Deficiency in language."
- It has been shown that when children enter school with less-than-adequate language skills, there is a 50 percent likelihood that they will encounter academic difficulties that will remain with them throughout the elementary years.
- Approximately 74 percent of three- to five-year-olds, or 6.8 million preschoolers, are in child care on a regular basis. A recent four-state study of eight hundred preschool children followed them from age four through the second grade. The study found that by second grade, a child's success in school is directly related to the quality of child care received during the preschool years.
- An in-depth study of the daily lives of one- to two-year-old children has found that differences in the amount of interaction between parents and their children translated into starkly different levels of later vocabulary development and IQ test scores—both indicators of a child's ability to succeed in school.

Some Illustrative Scenarios

It is the first week of kindergarten. Mrs. Dore is covering the unit on animals and preparing the children for an upcoming trip to the local zoo. Jeremy and Sam, both five years old, are seated next to each other on the floor. Jeremy eagerly anticipates the teacher's next question and shoots his hand up, waiting for a chance to speak. Sam is looking out the window, wondering whether or not it will be raining during outside playtime. Mrs. Dore forms the impression that Jeremy is bright and well adjusted; she makes a mental note to have the school psychologist observe Sam, who seems to have difficulty paying attention during group circle time and participating appropriately during class discussions.

Now let's flash back to some scenes from their early years:

- The first scene is the office of the local pediatrician, where both infants are in the waiting room with their mothers. Jeremy's mom has him seated on her lap, facing her. She is gently bouncing him and repeating the sounds he is producing: *"Bah, bah, bah, bah, bah!"* Sam is in a car seat/carrier placed on the floor. He is quietly staring around the waiting room and sucking on a pacifier. His mom is reading a magazine.

- Flash forward. They are two years old and having breakfast. Jeremy is seated in his booster seat at the table. He holds up his cup and says, "More juice!" Dad says, "You want more juice. Okay. You like to drink juice." Jeremy repeats, "Drink juice." Dad says, "We're drinking juice. After you finish your juice, we'll go to school." Jeremy says, "Go Mommy car!" Dad says, "Yes, you're going to school in Mommy's car. Mommy will drive you to school." Meanwhile, next door, Sam is seated in front of the TV, silently watching cartoons, eating a bowl of cereal while Mom is hurrying to get ready for them to leave the house. Holding up his cup, he says, "More juice!" Mom responds, "Not now, sweetie, we don't have time," then scoops him up and quickly puts on his jacket.

- And finally, at four years old, the boys are both waiting in an airport with their parents. Jeremy is sitting next to his dad. Dad is saying, "Okay, I'm thinking of an animal. It has a pocket to carry its baby in and can hop very fast. What is it?" Jeremy says, "Kangaroo! My turn!" One aisle over, Sam is sitting next to his mom, holding his Game Boy and silently pushing buttons. Mom is reading a magazine.

Hopefully it is obvious from these scenarios that Jeremy is receiving a much higher quality of language input and interaction. Now let's be clear: The point is not that you must be talking to your child incessantly, and you needn't feel neglectful if you spend your time in a waiting room reading a magazine. The intent of these scenarios is not to blame Sam's mother or to imply that she has caused his difficulties. The point is that these are examples of interaction moments—examples of how input can qualitatively differ.

Over time, the quality of interaction will affect language development for better or for worse. Better interactions will enhance language development.

Does Input (How I Talk to My Child) Matter?

The obvious question for parents and early-childhood educators is, Does quality of input *really* matter that much? Aren't children "hardwired" to pick up language anyway? We now have enough evidence to state with confidence that yes, input *does* matter. Because the human cortex is not fully developed at birth, the process of brain-cell development continues during the first years of life, and input plays an active and formative role in this process. The age-old debate regarding nature versus nurture is a false dichotomy, since nature (that is, the brain) is not a static entity but is actually shaped by the quality of nurturing it receives. The prevailing view in the 1970s and 1980s was that children were hardwired to learn language and that the quality of stimulation did not matter much. Now we know that stimulation begets growth, and therefore the quality of that stimulation can have either positive or negative outcomes. The evidence for this comes from several different fields of study.

Evidence From Scientific Research

In the field of neurology, studies of the brain are helping us appreciate its vast and complex interconnection of neurons. The development of these interconnections is at least partially related to, and dependent on, stimulation. As a child is seeing and touching an object and hearing the name of that object spoken, connections are being formed within the brain and actual physical changes are occurring on a cellular level. Nerve cells are establishing circuits that carry electrical impulses. This development of neurons and their connections to other neurons begins during the second trimester and continues well after birth. The brain at birth is only about one third the size of an adult's. From birth to about age four, brain weight increases fivefold. Myelinization—growth of the outer lining—of nerve cells in the human auditory cortex continues through about age twelve. Certain cells are predisposed for specialization within various areas of the brain, but the actual maturation of individual neurons and how they are interconnected is a work in progress for the developing infant.

In the field of linguistics, studies have looked at large groups of infants. The amount and quality of parent stimulation strongly correlate with the child's level of language development at a later stage. Betty Hart and Todd Risley, two experts in behavioral psychology and language development, have spent most of their professional lives exploring this question. Their recently published book, *Meaningful Differences,* provides a detailed account of their very thorough and painstaking research. They found that the amount and quality of interaction between parents and children have measurable long-term effects on vocabulary growth rate, vocabulary use, and IQ test scores.

Evidence From Cases of Deprivation

Fortunately, cases of extreme deprivation of early stimulation have been relatively rare. One such case was Genie, a child who was locked in a room for over ten years. Rescued in 1970 at the age of thirteen, she was placed in Children's Hospital in Los Angeles, California, where she underwent intense study and stimulation. At the time of her rescue, she could understand and speak only a few words. After intensive intervention, her vocabulary grew; however, her grammar remained severely disordered, lending support to the theory of a critical period for the development of language. This period is from birth to about age twelve. The movie *Nell* was based on another true-life situation, in which a developing child was deprived of any normal language model, since she was raised in the backwoods of Appalachia by a grandmother who apparently had suffered a stroke. Jodie Foster portrayed the distorted pronunciation and sentence structures of this child—it took a trained linguist to study her speech and decipher the sound patterns she was using. There have been other stories of such feral children as well, though these are less well documented. Studies of neglected infants institutionalized in Eastern Europe have shown not only language delays and difficulties but also more pervasive problems involving attachment and emotional development.

Evidence is also available from the babbling behavior of deaf children. In a sense, these children are deprived of input insofar as they are not able to hear sounds. A deaf infant will begin the babbling stage sounding similar to an infant with normal hearing. However, at about three to six months, when the normally hearing baby begins to experiment and play with the sounds he is producing (and hearing), the deaf infant will become more quiet, lacking the ability to hear his own sounds. In fact, at about ten months of age, a normally hearing baby's babbling typically shifts to consisting only of the sounds in the language that is being spoken to him. It is as if the auditory system is sifting out the important sound features of the language it will need and selectively discarding those that will not be necessary for speaking that language.

When Does Input Begin?

The auditory system develops during the third trimester of pregnancy. Research studies have shown that babies who heard their mothers' voices regularly before birth were actually able to distinguish her voice from others—and to prefer it—immediately after birth. A newborn's hearing system is ready and waiting to take in information. Infants only a few days old can discriminate between two highly different languages, and after about a month, they can detect subtle differences in specific language sounds, such as *p* and *b*.

What This Book Will Cover

It has become widely accepted among educators that language skills are important for school success and that input matters. The obvious next question is, How can we provide the best stimulation possible for language development to occur? That is the main question this book is designed to answer.

The book is divided into three parts. The first part, "Learning to Talk," will cover the specific features of language, both listening and speaking, that are expected to appear at various stages of a child's development. Each stage will be described in terms of typical behavior, what can be done to enhance development at that particular stage, and when to consult the advice of a speech-language pathologist. Part 2, "Talking Together," explains general principles and specific strategies that parents can use when talking with their children. The last part, "Talking to Learn," provides specific ways to help prepare a child for school success, as a participant in a classroom, and for learning to read.

Each of these sections is also available in a workshop format of one and a half hours each. They include videotaped segments illustrating the behaviors and techniques covered in the material, as well as role-playing activities.

I have tried to avoid the use of professional jargon, but there may be some terms that are unfamiliar to the reader. A glossary is provided at the end of the book.

What This Book Is *Not* Intended For

This book is not intended as a replacement for speech-language intervention. If you have concerns about your child's speech development, it is important to seek advice and professional assistance in order to determine if there is real cause for concern. So much assistance is available nowadays that it would be foolish to wait if you think your child might need help.

In addition, this book is not intended as a means for parents to hurry their child along in the belief that the earlier language develops, the better. Each child is capable of doing only what she is developmentally ready for. The quality of parent-child interaction will enhance that development, but speeding it up is neither necessary nor desirable. There may be some parents who would use the information in this book to obsessively monitor and control their child's language development. I would encourage them to read *The Hurried Child* by David Elkind.

Self-Check 1: Test Your Current Knowledge

See how much you already know about when children should be expected to be able to accomplish each of the language items below. [Source: Farber and

Goldstein, 1998; Reprinted with permission from the American Speech-Language-Hearing Association.] Read items 1 to 21. Place the number of each item where you think it belongs on the age chart at the bottom of the page. Remember, think about the average child.

1. Counts from one to ten
2. Says first word and names some objects
3. Knows idea of "yesterday" and "tomorrow"
4. Is able to give a short oral report
5. Points to pictures in a book
6. Fills in words or phrases in a familiar story (frequently heard book)
7. Retells a story using pictures from a book
8. Puts two words together when speaking and asks simple questions
9. Responds to requests such as "Come here"
10. Has a nine-hundred-word speaking vocabulary
11. Understands opposites such as "in and out," "on and off," and "top and bottom"
12. Understands "How much?" and "How long?"
13. Uses easily understandable speech
14. Predicts story endings
15. Understands prepositions and adjectives such as "big, little, on, in"
16. Plays simple games like pat-a-cake
17. Knows and names basic colors, sizes, and shapes
18. Points to body parts when someone names them (Show me _____.)
19. Knows days of week and months of year
20. Speaks in complete sentences
21. Relates events from the day

6-12 mos.	1-2 yrs.	2-3 yrs.	3-4 yrs.	4-5 yrs.	5-6 yrs.	6-7 yrs.

(Answers appear on the following page)

6-12 mos.	1-2 yrs.	2-3 yrs.	3-4 yrs.	4-5 yrs.	5-6 yrs.	6-7 yrs.
5	2	6	1	7	3	4
9	8	10	13	11	12	14
16	18	15	21	20	17	19

Part 1

Learning to Talk

Introduction

Congratulations! If you are reading this book you are probably a parent, a caregiver or an educator of young children—an awesome but highly rewarding situation to be in. *And* you are interested in how you talk with them. You may already realize how important your role is in your child's language development. What you may not realize, though, is that you can also make an enormous difference in the child's total development. And this book will help you make the most of your interactions with children and help prepare them for the demands of school.

Can You Hear Me Now? The Importance of Hearing

Any book on language development must include information about hearing, because a child can only learn to speak words he has heard spoken to him. What he will eventually say is the long-term outcome of the language that he has heard. A child who is not hearing well will be at high risk for problems in language development and later learning problems.

Photo: PNC / Brand X Pictures / Getty Images

Steven, a preschool child, was referred to me for auditory processing problems. The nursery school reported that his behavior was not good at school. He didn't pay attention and had a hard time following the rules. The teachers complained that "he just doesn't seem to listen or follow instructions." He was getting time-outs, but these were not proving to be effective. They were wondering if he had receptive language problems. Since there was no history of a hearing evaluation in his file, I referred his parents to an audiologist. On his next visit, Steven came in, plopped himself down in the small chair at the table, and announced, "Guess what? The doctor says I have a flute in my ear!" "A flute?" I said. "Ohhhh—*fluid!*" What the doctor had said was that Steven had fluid in his middle ear, a fairly common condition called otitis media. The speech Steven was hearing was muffled, and he was experiencing a moderate hearing loss. Of *course* he was becoming less interested in what people were saying to him—it was very hard work hearing the words. Listening to his teacher's words was like listening to a TV in a crowded room with the volume turned way down. He had tuned out.

What goes into a child's understanding a simple spoken sentence, such as "What's your name?" When sound strikes the eardrum (outer ear), the sound waves cause it to vibrate. These vibrations, in turn, cause three tiny bones, each attached to the next—in the space called the middle ear—to move back and forth. The last bone is attached to a tiny "window" in the cochlea, or inner ear. The cochlea can be thought of as a string of piano keys, curled up like a snail. The high "keys"—actually tiny hairlike nerve cells—pick up high-frequency sounds, and the low "keys" pick up low-frequency sounds. Here is a picture of what it looks like:

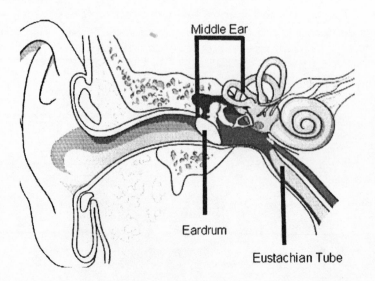

©2005 LifeArt. Lippincott Williams and Wilkins. All rights reserved.

After this it gets a lot more complicated. What happens between the cochlea and the brain, referred to as central auditory processing, is still a frontier area of exploration.

The signal passes several so-called stations, getting analyzed by groups of specialized cells along the way. These stations have names and locations, but the exact nature of what each does still eludes researchers. The final "stop" along the way consists of nerve cells located in different areas of the brain. Research has shown that as these cells are stimulated, they develop further, making more and more connections with other cells.

It is the ability of the brain to detect and finally make sense of these incoming signals that enables us to recognize and understand words, such as "What is your name?" But a lot goes into this seemingly simple act. First, we have to be paying attention to the words being spoken to us. We have to be able to distinguish the sounds being heard and to match them to the patterns of the sounds in the language we have been hearing and learning. The perception of spoken words— the ability to discriminate and recognize sounds—is only a portion of the job. When learning a foreign language, we have all experienced being able to repeat a foreign phrase verbatim and not have a clue as to what we have just said. We have to be able to retain the sounds in memory in order to process the sounds of the words, and we have to be able to connect the words formed by those connected sounds into the meanings that have been learned and stored—called association— in the brain. Then the meanings are subject to various interpretations, influenced by the situational expectations we have learned from our culture. When I ask a three-year-old child, "How are you?" and he responds "Three" instead of "Fine," it could mean that "How old are you?" has been asked of him so much that he has come to expect it from a grown-up he's talking with.

Like other parts of the brain, the auditory cortex, or the part of the brain that analyzes and derives meaning from sounds, begins developing during the last trimester of pregnancy and continues developing after birth. The infant brain is waiting to soak up spoken words, much like a computer hard drive that is deriving its operating system from the input it receives—the better the input, the better the operating system. Research has shown that from infancy through toddlerhood, children prefer sounds over visual materials when given a conflicting choice. In an experiment comparing adults and children, the groups were shown images paired with sounds and asked to remember these and to indicate when they occurred again. The images were then paired with different sounds, and the previously presented sounds were paired with different images. The adults almost always made their judgments based on the image—that is, they would pick a picture paired with another sound as having occurred before. More than half of the children, on the other hand, did the reverse—they judged correctness by the sound even when it conflicted with the picture. This preference for sound over pictures continues until approximately age five and is thought to be related to the importance that hearing plays in the development of language that takes place during this period.

A Word About Otitis Media, the Silent Crippler

Otitis media—the medical term for an inflammation or infection of the middle ear—is one of the most commonly occurring childhood conditions. It can reduce the hearing ability of the child, which can affect the development of the auditory system if the condition persists and is severe enough. Sometimes it can be silent, that is the child may feel no pain and run no fever.

Here's what happens: Fluid collects in the space that contains the three tiny bones that transfer the vibrations from the eardrum to the cochlea. This mass of liquid, which can become thick, interferes with the ability of the tiny bones to move back and forth and to transmit vibrations. Thus the signal to the cochlea is lost. (Hearing is not totally lost, however, since some sound vibrations still get through the bones of the skull.) If the signal coming in is not optimally detected, this can affect all of the processes that occur farther along the pathway.

Fortunately, postnatal hearing screening is becoming routine, so infants with hearing loss or deafness are identified early and receive intervention. Parents of newborns should make sure a screening has been done. Preschool children should be monitored for hearing problems and promptly screened if hearing difficulty is suspected. Children with frequent upper respiratory infections, whether they be colds or the result of allergies, are likely candidates for middle-ear fluid problems. Watch for such warning signs as the child turning up the TV, not responding when spoken to, appearing inattentive and disruptive, or asking "What?" frequently. Most pediatricians can easily perform a hearing screening as part of the routine medical checkup.

Now that we've made sure the hearing system is in place, we can begin looking at the miraculous process of speech and language development.

Chapter 1

Infancy: Crying, Cooing, Babbling, and First Words

Life is a flame that is always burning itself out,
but it catches fire again every time a child is born.
—George Bernard Shaw

It sometimes happens, even in the best of families, that a baby is born.
This is not necessarily cause for alarm.
The important thing is to keep your wits about you and borrow some money.
—Elinor Goulding Smith

"She was so quiet in there for all those nine months. Then we brought her home and all hell broke loose!" During the first several weeks of life, the baby is learning to physically adjust to life outside the womb. This is a stabilization period for the primary bodily functions of eating and sleeping, a period when some sort of general pattern or routine will be established for these functions. The primary goal is to learn to regulate such internal states as hunger and discomfort and to signal to caregivers the need for help. At this stage, the expressive communication consists of a cry (hopefully a good strong one). The cry during the first weeks is not something the baby does intentionally, however; it is purely an automatic response to some type of stress. It is designed to do one thing: help the infant survive.

Why Having a "Good" Baby Might Not Be So Good

The sound of a newborn crying can be very unnerving. It can wake a deep-sleeping parent and make anyone within earshot feel a sense of urgency. Yet the ability to produce a strong cry is an important early sign that a baby is healthy. The cry is the first form of communication, and with a responsive adult around, babies quickly come to learn just how powerful it can be. The muscles and coordination used in a wailing cry are the very same as those used later for what is known as speech breathing. When we talk, we generally take in a short inhalation and speak on a controlled exhalation, using the air as it moves through our vibrating vocal cords. In crying, the same pattern is going on: a quick inhalation followed by a long wail. Development of upper-body, or trunk-muscle, strength and control is essential for the ability to produce speech. If we tend to think of a "good" baby as one that does not cry often, we may be ignoring an important sign of positive development.

Toward the end of the three-month period, we begin to hear some cooing. This usually takes place during periods of calm, when more primary needs, like hunger, have been satisfied. Cooing is basically a vowel sound, resembling an open *ooh* or *ahh*. Research has shown that babies are tuned in to hearing a response to these sounds at as young as three months of age. If the baby hears a human voice in response, she may produce another sound and wait, showing an alert, still pause, listening for another response. These primitive and rudimentary "conversations" are the earliest examples of turn taking, an important skill in learning to verbally interact with others. Babies at this age will also show their pleasure and interest in human attention by wriggling, widening their eyes, moving their limbs in a generalized form of excitement, and smiling.

How can we tell that a baby is hearing? One indication that the hearing system is working is the startle reflex, which a baby exhibits when a loud noise, such as a sharp clap, is produced. A baby will also show signs of listening by becoming still when there are voices nearby.

By six months, a shift from cooing to babbling emerges. Babbling is the production of the various sounds, or phonemes, that a language is made up of. Every language has a set of phonemes, some of which will not exist in other languages. This is what makes it hard for an adult to learn a foreign language, since we are not accustomed to hearing or producing the phonemes that are unfamiliar to us. Initially, the child produces all types of sounds, even those that are not in the language being spoken around him. But babies learn to discriminate and produce—as early as nine months—the phonemes in their own language, and their babbling shifts to sounds that exist only within the language (or languages) they are hearing. These are the sounds they will continue to produce and that will later form the basis of their spoken language.

Importance of Babbling

The ability to speak is directly related to the developing ability of the child to move the muscles of the tongue, lips, and jaw in increasingly controlled ways. In infancy, the child begins this important journey through babbling, making sounds and syllables in various rhythms, intonations, and combinations.

The importance of the babbling stage has become increasingly appreciated. Children spend many hours (hopefully) in playful rehearsal of a variety of consonants and vowels, gaining control over the production of sounds and matching up what they are hearing to what they are doing with their mouths. This repertoire of phonemes becomes refined and, at a certain point, unique to and consistent with the phonemic system of the language (or languages) that the child has been hearing. Once again, the notion of a quiet baby being a "good" baby is erroneous. In fact, the absence of or limited babbling during this period can be an early signal that there may be a problem, either with the ability to hear sounds or with the motoric ability to produce them.

Should I Be Talking to My Baby at This Stage? It Feels Kind of Silly

Absolutely you should be talking to your baby at this stage. Although he does not comprehend the words, he is learning the sounds and intonation patterns of the language being spoken to him and learning to discriminate the voices of the important people in his life. His brain is busy mapping and categorizing sounds that he will later be able to produce. Many adults automatically change their speech patterns when talking to very young infants, and this helps accentuate the very aspects that the child is picking up on—the speech is usually slightly slower, with exaggerated intonation.

Also, the clearer the signal, the better your baby will be able to benefit from hearing language. Research has shown that children whose mothers have the highest speech clarity tend to do better on measures of their speech perception. So go ahead and talk (and speak clearly!). Your baby loves to hear your voice!

Does a Noisy Environment Make a Difference?

A recent study conducted at the University of California at San Francisco has shown that exposure to continuous white noise negatively affects the development of the auditory region of the brain, which may hinder the development of both hearing and language. The study was conducted on rats, but the principle is the same for humans. It is important that the speech a baby hears is as clear as possible, and lots of constant background noise will probably be a hindrance. It's a good idea to spend time interacting with your baby away from a noisy environment.

Can't the Baby Pick Up the Information From Watching TV or a Video?

The short answer to this question is no. It seems that babies have a strong preference for real people. They also have a preference for hearing sounds rather than seeing pictures. But the sounds are most effective when coming from a real human voice. There have been studies that compared how well babies learned to discriminate sounds when exposed to videos versus live human speech. A study conducted at the Center for Mind, Brain, and Learning at the University of Washington, led by neuroscientist Patricia Kuhl, compared two groups of nine-month-old infants. One group was exposed to Mandarin Chinese spoken by live people (native Mandarin speakers), while the other group was exposed to the same material via a DVD or audiotape. The group exposed to the live speakers was able to distinguish phonetic elements of that language, but the group watching the DVD or listening to the tape could not. Television does not provide the quality of input that live human interaction does. A TV can't respond to the sounds a baby is making. There is no *inter*action. And human communication is all about *interaction*. You talk, I listen, and then I talk while you listen. That is the pattern of conversation. If a baby's sounds are not responded to, which a TV cannot do, this important step is missing and will have a negative effect on the development of speech.

On the Verge of First Words

At about nine months, there is a qualitative shift in the type of babbling a baby produces. One of the new qualities is the repetition of consonant-vowel combinations, such as *bah, bah, bah, bah,* or *di, di, di, di.* This is called reduplicated babbling and usually indicates that the child is on the threshold of saying his first true word. Another new aspect to the babbling is that if the parent babbles a sound combination in the child's repertoire, such as *bah, bah,* the child can now imitate it back to the parent. The child may also show clear understanding of some words, such as "no," his own name, or the names of family members. He may be able to produce gestured words, such as waving bye-bye or putting his hands up for "so big." Babies do a lot of communicating at this stage just by vocalizing in combination with looking and reaching. They can "comment" by showing or giving an object to the adult. They can request items by pointing or reaching and vocalizing. They can show clear rejection by turning the head and pushing items away while vocalizing displeasure. Interactive repetitive games, such as peekaboo and pat-a-cake, are typically highly enjoyable, since the child is able to indicate his desire to repeat the routine over again. As a point of interest, research in sign language acquisition has shown that gestured words can be learned earlier than spoken ones. Babies can learn to sign words with their hands before they learn to speak the words.

First Words

The milestone of first spoken words, which usually occurs at approximately one year of age, is no small accomplishment. The child has spent much of the first year touching, feeling, and exploring objects, learning that if an object is turned around, it remains the same, and if it is dropped (or thrown!) out of sight, it still exists. This stage of mental development is called object permanence. If an object that a child is looking at is covered by a small cloth, the child that has achieved object permanence will typically remove the cloth to retrieve the object. With this mental concept mastered, the child is ready to grasp the notion of reference—that a word or a particular spoken sound pattern can refer to a particular object or action. It was this breakthrough that was depicted in the story of Helen Keller when she made the connection between the running water and the pattern her teacher, Anne Sullivan, was tracing on her palm. Now the child is opened up to a whole different world, in which things can be referred to by a pattern of sounds she can make with her mouth. The child has learned to control the syllables that have previously been practiced in babbling, so that now the random repetition of *"dah, dah, dah, dah"* has magically turned into "Dada" when Daddy appears. Correspondingly, the child can now respond to simple requests for various objects, such as "give me the cup" or "where's your shoe?"

Ages and Stages

[Sources for this and other Ages and Stages Charts: Anderson, R.M., Miles, M. and Matheny, P.A., 1963; Gard, A., Gilman, L. and Gorman, J., 1993; Westby, C., 1988]

From Cooing and Babbling to First Words

Zero to Three Months (stabilization period)

Receptive	Expressive	Motor
Reacts to sudden noises	Strong cry	Visually alert
Heeds spoken voices	Begins to vocalize sounds	Successful feeding pattern established
	Meaningful smile	Physically responsive

Six Months

Receptive	Expressive	Motor
Localizes sound source	Laughs aloud	Good head balance
Turns to speaking voice	Babbles several sounds on one breath	Gaining sitting posture
	Cooing—>Babbling	Picks up a spoon

Nine Months

Receptive	Expressive	Motor
Understands "no, no"	Waves "bye-bye"	Feeds self small dry food
Understands and responds to name	Babbles extensively	Grasps and pulls
	Reduplicated babbling	Plays peekaboo
Listens to and imitates sounds	Imitative babbling	
	Communicates through intonation	Enjoys playful routines such as pat-a-cake

One Year

Receptive	Expressive	Motor
Listens with understanding to words	First meaningful words	Good chewing, sucking, and swallowing movements
Follows simple requests: "Give it to me," "Get the ____"	Imitates a variety of sounds	Stands without support
Understands gestures	Attempts new words	Opens a small box

Play Behavior

0-3 months. It is difficult to play with a newborn, as many a disappointed older sibling has learned. However, newborns are busy developing the visual and motor skills that will enable them to have fun exploring and interacting with the world. As discussed above, this is a period of stabilization, in which they are getting acclimated to life outside the womb. When not crying or sleeping, they may spend periods of time simply staring, or gazing. The hands are predominantly closed, with no reaching out to grasp objects, though newborns will grasp objects placed in their hands. They will raise the head up to look around when lying on their stomach.

3-6 months. Now she will add some new behaviors. She will work at getting an object that is out of reach and will start to wriggle with pleasure at the sight of it. Once an object is in her hand, she will put it in her mouth or bang it on a table. She watches her hands as if discovering how they can move. She will look at and shake a rattle.

6-9 months. Motor skills have developed enough that she is now able to explore objects with her fingers instead of just grasping them with the entire hand. She still likes to explore them with her mouth as well. She will be taking in more of the world around her as she sits without support, pulls herself to a standing position, and crawls.

9-12 months. In addition to exploring with her hands, feeling, and tasting objects, she now begins to deliberately drop them and watch them fall, to the exasperation of adults and the endless entertainment of older siblings. She will squeeze or poke objects to hear the noise they make and enjoys putting objects in containers and taking or dumping them out again. Watch out, she also will begin to throw intentionally but has little control of the direction!

Some General Principles to Keep in Mind for This Age

- Talk frequently to your child, but keep utterances relatively short, clear, and somewhat repetitive.
- Say what the child sees—that is, talk about whatever the child is focusing on.
- Imitate their babbling sounds back to them and pause, waiting for them to take a turn.
- Treat any sounds the child makes as a communicative turn (even burps!), and respond as though you are continuing a conversation.
- Create a stimulating situation, such as making a wind-up toy move, approaching the child playfully with a stuffed animal, or just bouncing him on your knee; then stop and wait to see if he indicates that he wants more.

- Since daily routine is the skeleton on which language is fleshed out, create language-learning situations out of dressing, eating, and bathing by simply labeling the objects and actions and talking as you go.

Photo: Mark Andersen / Rubberball Productions / Getty Images

Oral-Motor Development:
From Sucking to Chewing and Drinking

This is a good place to discuss oral-motor development, since so much change takes place in how the mouth works in the first two years of a child's life.

Sucking, Swallowing, and Chewing

Newborns are "suckers" in the literal sense of the word. Infants are born with the ability to suck (hence the term "sucking reflex"), and their mouths are well designed little sucking machines. The lips seal on to the nipple of the breast or bottle, and the tongue moves back and forth. Anyone who has attempted to feed an infant his first solid food will remember the tongue pushing the food right back out, since the tongue can basically move only forward and backwards. This is called a suckle swallow. This suck-swallow pattern gradually shifts once the child has teeth and begins chewing solid food, until, at about the age of four to six years, a mature adult pattern of swallowing is fully developed. In a normal adult swallow, the tip of the tongue is placed on the alveolar ridge, located behind the upper front teeth. Then the food, which has been chewed and collected on the middle of the tongue, is pushed toward the back of the throat in a wavelike motion. Once the child has teeth and begins to chew solid food, usually at around twelve months of age, the tongue develops lateral control, enabling movement of food sideways, from the molars on one side of the mouth to those on the other side. This lateral control helps the sides of the tongue become able to stabilize against the molars during speech, enabling differentiated movement of the tongue tip. Tongue-tip movements eventually become more refined and precise, allowing the development of the more highly coordinated tongue-tip sounds involving controlled airflow, such as *s, z* and *sh,* which are the later sounds to develop.

Avoid Prolonged Bottle Use

If a child is allowed to use a bottle or pacifier past the eruption of the full set of baby teeth, the suckle-swallow pattern may be prolonged, and the development of differentiated tongue movements may become delayed. Children with delayed development in the oral musculature will be at risk for delays and difficulty with articulation of sounds. Allowing a baby to fall asleep with a bottle can lead to severe tooth decay. Also, drinking from a bottle while lying down can enable liquid to enter the eustachian tubes—the tiny tubes that connect the back of the throat to the middle-ear cavity—making the baby more susceptible to ear infections. Doctors advise bidding good-bye to the bottle between twelve and fifteen months of age. If your child has gotten attached to the bottle as a source of comfort, the longer you wait, the harder it will be to wean him off it. Here are some helpful suggestions:

- Help your child pick out her own special cup, perhaps one with a favorite color or character on it; praise the child for drinking the new, grown-up way.
- Gradually introduce greater proportions of water to the juice in the bottle so that drinking it will have less appeal, or, better yet, fill it only with water.
- Adopt a cups-only rule at mealtime.
- Acknowledge the child's feelings if the child becomes angry or frustrated, but stand your ground.
- If the child is used to taking the bottle to bed, prepare a special snack to have before bedtime so that he will feel full, or substitute a soft cuddly toy for comfort.

Mouthing of Objects

One of the ways an infant explores the world is through his mouth. Mouthing of objects is not only common, it is also desirable for children under the age of one. At this age, children seek the sensory experience of touch and taste, using their lips, tongues, and jaws to explore the objects around them. The stimulation they receive through this type of exploration is a necessary part of development. Mouthing of objects also helps develop the muscles of the lips, tongue, and jaw, which will contribute to food chewing and swallowing and to speech development. Safe and appropriate objects to explore should be provided. These might include teething toys, toothbrushes, metal spoons, and dry washcloths.

Promoting Good Oral-Motor Habits

- By one year, the child should be able to chew small bits of food such as Cheerios; do not allow the child to stuff large amounts of food into his mouth, since this can result in choking.
- When spoon-feeding, keep the spoon size appropriate for the child's mouth, and encourage the use of the lips in sweeping food from the spoon.
- Discontinue the use of a bottle as soon as the child is able to drink from a cup. Prolonged use of a bottle may result in bottle mouth, a condition wherein the tongue is in a chronic forward position and the front upper and lower teeth may no longer meet and overlap but rather develop an open-bite type of pattern, in which when the child bites the back teeth together, there remains an opening between the upper and lower front teeth where the bottle is typically placed. All objects that are suckled for prolonged periods of time, including bottles, pacifiers, fingers, and blankets, will interfere with the neuromuscular development of the tongue and can create problems with teeth, lips, and tongue and, consequently, with speech.
- Avoid pacifiers after one year of age. If using one, make sure the pacifier is of the contoured variety so as not to interfere with the position of teeth that are growing in. Use of pacifiers during the first few years of life has been shown to be associated with the development of a crossbite—misalignment of the upper and lower teeth.
- Use travel cups sparingly and not at all if the child seems to be maintaining a suckle style of swallow. Straw pop-up cups are much better—Playtex makes a good one. Make sure the straw is short enough so that it doesn't rest on the tongue, but only on the lips. You can cut the soft pop-up straw down to approximately a quarter-inch to half-inch length.

- Be alert to a chronic open-mouth posture, which is when the child's mouth is open at rest. This posture is characterized by a tongue-forward resting position, resulting in weakening of the jaw musculature and delayed development of tongue-tip coordination and can contribute to articulatory problems, such as lisping. This type of posture is usually associated with chronic upper respiratory infections and/or enlarged tonsils and adenoids.
- Provide safe and appropriate objects for the child to explore with his mouth.

Top Ten Activities for Children Three Months to One Year of Age

1. **Sounds Around (Sound Localization).** Use an object that makes a distinctive sound: cellophane, keys, rattle. Place the child in an infant seat. Show him the object and demonstrate the noise it makes. Let him hold it and make the noise. Then stand slightly behind the child and hold the object out to one side then the other—the child should turn to localize the sound. Then return the object to the child and talk to him while he holds it again.

2. **Can You Copy? (Contingent Responding).** Hold the child in your lap so he is facing you. Begin talking to him. Pause and wait. The child may make some vowel-like sounds, such as *ahhh*. Repeat this sound back to him, and then stop and wait for him to make another sound. A later-developing version of this game is to produce a babbling sound that you have heard your child make before, such as *bah, bah, bah,* and then wait. The child may respond by imitating you. Keep the turns going!

3. **Peekaboo.** Cover your face with your hands, a scarf, or a napkin. Say, "Where's Mommy?" Wait a few seconds, then pull the cloth away and say, "Peekaboo! I see you!" If the child responds positively, repeat. Try waiting with your face covered and see if the child will attempt to pull the covering away. Then cover the child's face and say, "Where's [name]?"

4. **Hide-and-Seek.** Allow the child to watch you slowly move out of sight. Call her name and see if she looks for you (sneak a peek). Then come back into sight and say, "Here I am!" You can also try this game with a toy by moving the toy out of sight by covering it or putting it behind another object. Then ask, "Where's the bear?" Help the child retrieve the object, saying, "Here's the bear!"

5. **Spoon to Mouth.** Place several mouthable objects—mouthing toys, spoons, and the like—in front of the child. Try to use a variety of sizes and textures. Talk while the child explores each object.

6. **In and Out.** Using a clear plastic tennis-ball container, drop a favorite small object in the container, saying, "In the can!" Then shake the container and allow the child to hold and shake the container. Help the child dump out the object and say, "Out!" or "Whee!" with exaggerated intonation.

7. **All Fall Down.** Using blocks or cardboard boxes, place each block or box on top of another one, saying, "Up, up," and continue until all are stacked. Help the child knock them down, saying, "Uh-oh, they fell down!"

8. **Bang, Bang.** Using a toy hammer or wooden spoon, show the child how to bang, saying, "Bang, bang!" Place a few metal pots or bowls in front of the child and help her bang these.

9. **Whoops!** With the child sitting in a high chair, place a few small interesting objects on the tray. Slowly move one to the edge and allow it to fall over, saying, "Whoops, where's your block?" See if the child looks over the tray to find the object. If not, point and say, "Oh look, there's your block!" Retrieve the object and give it to the child. Help the child push it over the edge herself.

10. **Uh-oh!** With the child sitting in a high chair, tie an object (for example, a rattle) to the chair with a string. Push the rattle off the tray and say, "Uh-oh, where's the rattle?" Then pull up the string and retrieve the object, saying, "Here's the rattle!"

With many of the preceding activities, you can wait after an action has been completed to see if the child indicates to you, even nonverbally, that he wants the activity repeated. At this point, you can say the word "more" or "again" with a rising intonation, then falling intonation as you repeat the activity.

Songs and Chants

One of the most effective things to do with an infant is perhaps the simplest of all. It requires no special gadgets or things to buy and has been part of the human experience for who knows how long. A simple song or chant, whether one you learned as a child or one you make up spontaneously, will provide a source of great pleasure. It doesn't matter if you can't carry a tune—the baby will not be judging you. The combination of being held, rocked, bounced, or sung to is a powerful, loving act. Whatever simple tune you know, such as "Twinkle, Twinkle, Little Star," "Row, Row, Row Your Boat," or "Mary Had a Little Lamb," will work fine. Try to make up a song or chant using the baby's name. I remember chanting to the tune of "It's Raining, It's Pouring," substituting my son's name: "Daniel, Daniel, time to go to beddie." One of my fondest memories of my grandfather is having been bounced on his knees to "Ol' Dan Tucker was a fine old man ..." or "Oh, Susannah, don't you cry for me."

Books to Buy or Borrow and Suggestions for Using Them

Most experts agree that a child's love of books can and should begin in infancy. Even if the baby isn't actually comprehending many of the words, the auditory parts of his developing brain will be absorbing the sound patterns he hears, and he will be connecting books and spoken words with the pleasure of interacting with you.

The following are a few favorites that appear on many lists of suggested books for children.

For the under eight-months age group, look for books that have rhythm and rhyme. You can move your body to the beat, and your baby will enjoy the intonation and patterns of your voice. Here are a few books that are ideal for this:

> *Play Rhymes* by Marc Brown
> *Good Night, Moon* by Margaret Wise Brown
> *Rosie's Walk* by Pat Hutchins
> *Read-Aloud Rhymes for the Very Young* by Jack Prelutsky
> *Tomie DePaola's Mother Goose* by Tomie DePaola
> *My First Mother Goose* by Rosemary Wells

By eight months, you can begin to introduce form-board books (books with hard boardlike pages) that have simple pictures of real objects. They are sturdy and will not be easily torn when the baby reaches out to grab (or taste!) the page. These lend themselves to pointing out and repeating individual words in such phrases as "Look, there's a ball. The ball is big. That's a big ball." Your baby will want to begin holding the book himself and trying to turn the pages and will soon learn to elicit the names of pictured items from you by pointing and waiting for you to name an item or pointing and saying something like "Dah?" Other useful books are those with very little text and lots of pictures. Some have actual objects or textures for the child to feel. Allow your child time to explore the book and to initiate an action or utterance that you can then respond to. Try the following:

> *Moon Bear* by Frank Asch
> *Where's Spot?* by Eric Hill
> *Mama, Do You Love Me?* by Barbara Joose
> *Peter's Chair* by Ezra Jack Keats
> *Pat the Bunny* by Dorothy Kunhardt
> *Clap Hands* by Helen Oxenbury
> *"More, More, More," Said the Baby* by Vera Williams

Choose books that you enjoy. In her book *How to Get Your Child to Love Reading* Esme Raji Codell provides many useful ideas and lists of books for all ages. The number one hint on her list is "Love the book yourself before you read it to the children." Another helpful hint is "Read with expression." In other words, don't be shy. Ham it up!

Infancy can and should be the starting point for a daily read-aloud time. Remember that the goal is pleasurable interaction involving you, the book, and the baby—however that happens. So relax and have fun!

Chapter 2

Age One to Two: Walking and Talking

To help your children turn out well,
spend twice as much time with them and half as much money.
—H. Jackson Brown

You can learn many things from children.
How much patience you have, for instance.
—Franklin P. Jones

The growth in the number of words a child uses is slow at first. But one word can do so much! The child's first twenty words usually refer to familiar people, objects, or events in the his life and play an important role in daily activities. Baby Jason is sitting in his high chair and has dropped his bottle. "Baba!" he whines. He later sees inside the refrigerator and notices his bottle. "Baba!" he says, pointing to the bottle. When being put to bed, he is looking at a picture book showing a baby with a bottle. "Baba?" he asks, pointing at the bottle. When he uses the word "Dada," he could mean "That's Daddy's car" or "There's Daddy" or "Is Daddy coming?" or "Pick me up, Daddy!" Each of these has been the same word, but in each situation the word was being used to convey a different meaning. Other typical first words are ones that accomplish an important function for the child, such words as "more," "up," and "down." Words are usually produced in a simplified form, typically a single consonant and a vowel.

Also common at this stage is the use of jargon. Jargon is like babbling but a more sophisticated form. It consists of sounds strung together that resemble real sentences, because the child is using intonation patterns. Interspersed in these strings can be real words. My own son at this stage, attempting to ask for milk, produced something that sounded like "Ladaladalada, milk"!

Ages and Stages

Cracking the Code/Walkin' and Talkin'

Twelve to Eighteen Months

Receptive	Expressive	Motor
Follows simple one-step commands	Uses most vowels and consonants in jargon	Continual walking activities
Points to recognized objects	Repeats words heard	Begins awkward running
	Uses three to twenty words	Beginning to feed self with spoon
	Answers "What's this?"	
		Imitates a two- to three-block tower
	Words have consonant-vowel structure (*bo* for "boat")	

Another feature of the words used at this stage is that they are often overextended in their use. For example, a child who learns the word "dog" as the label for the family pet may assume that this word must refer to any four-legged creature. Later, upon seeing a picture of a goat or a horse, the child may produce "dog." This can make for some humorous situations. One woman was having a formal ladies' luncheon. The mailman rang the bell to hand-deliver a package. When she opened the door, to her embarrassment, her child announced, "Dada!"

Play Behavior

By this age, the child has come to associate objects with their functions or actions. For example, if given a crayon and paper, she may attempt to scribble on the paper. Similarly, she will imitate other actions, such as sweeping with a toy broom or putting a comb through her hair. She tends to play in a solitary way but will look on as another child plays.

An important way to be helpful to your child at this age is simply to tune in to what she is focusing on and to say an appropriate word or phrase simply and clearly. The key is to remain totally in the present moment, since that is where the child is. For example, if the child is examining an object, name the object a few times. It is good to look at simple picture books in which there are clear examples of objects. Tell your child to "find the _____." You may hear your child ask you what things are by saying something like "Uh dah?" or simply "Dah" while pointing to a picture and looking at you, waiting for a response. You can then answer, "That's a _____."

At this stage, children love rhymes and songs, especially ones that involve body movement and physical contact, such as "This Little Piggy Went to Market," "Itsy Bitsy Spider," or "Pat-a-Cake." The singsong quality and repetitive nature of these traditional nursery rhymes make them ideal for language development at this age. Once your child is familiar with a rhyme, try leaving off the last word of a line, such as "Pat-a-cake, pat-a-cake, baker's . . ." and help your child to fill in the missing word. This is a common technique used by teachers and can also be used with repetitive and highly predictable storybooks once the child is a little older.

Putting Words Together

Eighteen to Twenty-four Months

Receptive	Expressive	Motor
Points to body parts	Vocabulary growth spurt (two-hundred-plus words)*	Turns pages singly
Can "Show me a _____."		Imitates circular motion with a pencil
	Two-word sentences	
Answers simple questions, such as "What is your name?" "What does the doggy say?"	begin e.g., "Mommy car" (meaning may vary with situation)	Makes tower of three to four blocks
	Expresses existence, recurrence, rejection, etc.	Walks, runs fairly well
		Kicks a large ball

* There is a wide range of normal at this stage. Some precocious two-year-olds are carrying on conversations and are putting several words together in a sentence. A general rule of thumb is that by two years of age, a child should have a working vocabulary of at least fifty words.

Once the child has achieved approximately a fifty-word vocabulary, two-word sentences begin to appear, although single words will still predominate. When the ability to combine words has emerged, there is usually a noticeable growth spurt in vocabulary. At this point, new words are being quickly acquired. This is a time when input is especially important, since the child can only acquire a word that she hears spoken by someone around her. In a well-known study described in their book *Meaningful Differences*, Hart and Risley studied the daily interactions of one- and two-year-old children and their parents. What they found was that differences in the amount of time parents spent talking with their children directly related to corresponding differences in the extent of the children's vocabulary.

By two years of age, a child is able to produce in words what he has been busily discovering by touching, holding, mouthing, turning, and, much to the exasperation of tired parents, repeatedly dropping. He is now able to talk about what he has learned about the world. Lois Bloom and Margaret Lahey, whose classic text has been widely used in the training of speech-language pathologists, created categories to describe these early notions:

- Existence—that there are various objects in the world and that each of them has a name, for example, "der a ball" ("there's the ball")
- Recurrence—that things can happen and then happen again, or that things can be eaten or drunk and then replaced, as when the child finishes his juice and says, "More juice"
- Rejection—that we can choose to reject objects that are offered to us or to reject actions that we do not want to do, as when offered another cookie, the child may say "No cookie," or when it is time to take a bath, "No bath"
- Disappearance—that objects can go out of sight or be eaten up, as in "all gone"
- Possession—that objects can belong to people, as in "Mommy car;" "mine," "my shoe"
- Denial—that we can disagree with statements made by others, as when Mommy says, "I think we need to change you; your diaper is wet," and the child says, "Not wet"
- Action—"eat," "go"
- Location—"up," "down," "here," "there"
- Attribution—that objects have features that distinguish them from similar objects, as in "red ball," "big ball"

The child is also learning that the order of the words matters: the person doing the action comes before the name of the action and the person or thing being acted upon comes after the action. "Daddy kick" and "Kick Daddy" are two very different realities with very different outcomes! Word-order rules will vary depending on the language a child is learning. For example, while babies in America are learning that adjectives precede the objects they are describing ("red ball"), babies across the ocean in France are learning the opposite—that the object generally comes first and the adjective second, as in *"bal rouge."*

Questions begin to appear but are produced as a word or phrase with rising intonation: "Go?" "Go car?" "Daddy eat?"

Play Behavior

In the same way that the child is able to put two words together to express a relationship between objects and actions or between people and objects, she is able to reflect this understanding in her play. For example, she may perform certain actions, such as washing, feeding, or combing the hair, not only on herself but also on a doll. Stacking and knocking down blocks is another favorite, as are sand, rice, and water play, wherein she enjoys the repetitions of filling, pouring, and dumping out.

The child doesn't yet truly engage in play *with* peers, but does what is called parallel play. He plays near or next to others, but not with them. He may talk to himself as he plays. Some social interaction with peers will take place in the form of hugs or, if things aren't going well, in less socially acceptable behaviors, such as pushing, grabbing objects away from others, or even pulling hair and kicking. The two-year-old will have a ways to go to become a well-behaved social being ready to present himself to the world of school.

Photo: SW Productions / Brand X Pictures / Getty Images

Some General Principles to Keep in Mind About This Age

- Continue to follow the child's lead in what is being talked about, but keep your rate slower than you would normally use, and remember to speak clearly, repeating and exaggerating the names of items the child is focused on.
- When the child initiates communication by saying a word or phrase, take the opportunity to respond contingently. (More specifics will be provided in the next section.) This means that you respond by saying something that relates to the child's words and ideas. You can also expand his utterances by fleshing out the words into a more grammatically complete sentence. For example, CHILD: "Cookie fall down." ADULT: "Yes, the cookie fell on the floor. We can't eat it. It's dirty."
- Continue to base communication on the immediate context and focus on what the child is doing or interested in.
- Joint book reading can be a highly language-stimulating activity. Allow the child to lead by pointing and requesting you to name items.

Saying It Right: Phonology and Biology

There is great variation in the clarity of toddlers' speech. Part of this has to do with the physical maturation of the anatomy—that is, control over the muscle movements of the lips, tongue, and jaw. The other part has to do with the acquisition of the phonological rules. Phonology refers to the sounds, or phonemes, that make up a language. For example, a child who says "sink" for "think" and "thee" for "see" clearly can produce the phonemes *s* and *th* but has not yet fully acquired the rules for using them.

The development of speech sounds is directly related to the maturation of the entire oral-motor system. This is a fairly lengthy and involved progression with a few main themes.

Increasingly Dissociated Movements of Jaw, Lips, and Tongue

In infancy, the tongue, lips, and jaw are undifferentiated from one another and tend to move together. The earliest consonants to develop are *m*, *p*, *b*, *n*, *d*, *w*, and *h*. These are all sounds that can be made with relatively simple movements of the jaw, lips, and tongue, with the jaw movement doing much of the work. For example, the words "Mama" or "Baba" or "Dada" can be made by basically opening and closing the jaw. Gradually the jaw movements become more refined, and the lips and tongue move more independently to produce a more adultlike version, in which these words can be produced with little or no jaw movement.

Differentiation of the lips from the jaw enables the production of such sounds as *w*, as well as increased control over lip sounds, such as *p*, *b*, and *m*. Differentiating between nasal and oral airflow creates the distinction between such consonants as *m* and *b*, and *n* and *d*. Control over voice-onset time creates the difference between some consonants, such as *b* and *p*. From a purely physical standpoint, it makes sense that these early-developing phonemes are the ones most frequently used during the first two years.

Successful mastery of front versus back tongue movements enables the child to develop the back consonants *k* and *g*, differentiating them from the front consonants *t* and *d*. This ability emerges between two and four years of age. Hence it would not be unusual to hear a two-year-old say "dawdie" for "doggie."

Fine Motor Development and Control of Tongue Positions and Movement

Control of airflow and combinations of contact enable the production of friction sounds, or fricatives, such as *sh*, *ch*, *s*, *z*, and *v*. These demand more refined control of articulatory movements and develop somewhat later, with a large range in the ages at which they are acquired. They require fine-motor movements of the tongue tip operating separately from other parts of the tongue, in much the same way as fine-motor finger movements require differentiation of fingers from hands, and hands from arms.

Sounds that generally take the longest to develop are *r*, *l*, *s*, and *th*, and it is not uncommon for many children to enter kindergarten with these sounds not fully mastered. These sounds require the most refined and highly developed motor control of the tongue.

Is My Child's Articulation Normal for His Age?

It is often hard for parents to determine whether their child's sound errors are perfectly normal or a sign that there may be a problem. The general rule of thumb is the law of fourths—that by two, the child's speech should be intelligible roughly half the time; by three, speech should be three-quarters intelligible to familiar listeners, and by four, speech should be fully intelligible with some sound errors still expected.

Top Ten Activities for Children One to Two Years of Age

1. **Songs and Chants That Involve Movement.** These are a big hit at this age. Typical ones include "This Little Piggie," "If You're Happy and You Know It," "Eensie Weensie Spider," and "The Wheels on the Bus." If

some songs are unfamiliar, your local bookstore will have many picture-book versions and music CDs to help you out.

2. **What's That Noise?** Collect several objects that make noise. These might include keys that jingle, a party horn, cellophane, a rattle, a toy phone, or a bell. Using a tape recorder, record the sound of each object, separated by a long pause. With the child seated, place the objects on the table in front of him, then play the tape. When a noise is heard, say, "What's that?" Pause the tape, find the object, and allow the child to make the noise. Then label the object, saying, "That's the bell. The bell is ringing."

3. **Down on the Farm.** Collect several small toy farm animals: a cow, pig, chicken, duck, or horse. Take one of the animals and make the sound of the animal; for example, move the cow and say, "*Moooo!* The cow says *mooo!*" Make the cow walk to your child and leave it there; wait for him to pick it up and explore it. Repeat with each of the other animals. Later on, you can just make one of the sounds and see if the child can find the animal on his own. For example, say, "*Mooo!* Who says *moo?*" Then help your child find the cow.

4. **What's in There?** Take several containers of different sizes with tops that can be removed (small boxes, margarine tubs, and so forth), and place a small interesting object in each. Take one object and shake it, saying, "I wonder what's in there!" The child will probably try and reach for the container. Say, "You want the box. Here's the box." As the child tries to open the box, say, "Open. Open the box." Help the child open it, and say, "What's that? It's a ____!" Repeat with the other containers.

5. **Balloon Fun.** Blow up a balloon. Help the child bat the balloon up in the air, saying, "Up, up, up—the balloon is going up." As the balloon comes down, say, "Down, down—the balloon is coming down." Or simply blow the balloon bigger and bigger, and then on the count of three, let the balloon fly around the room. Your child will be very amused at the wacky movements and places where the balloon ends up. You can say, "Where is it? It's under the table!" (Cautionary note: Balloons can be a choking hazard. Don't let the child play with a balloon unsupervised.)

6. **Beach Bag.** Place several objects inside a large tote or beach bag one at a time. Name each object as you pick it up. Then say, "Bye-bye. ____ is all gone!" as you help the child put it in the bag. Then let the child dump the objects out of the bag again and start over.

7. **Bubble Fun.** Get a jar of bubbles. Say the word "bubbles" a few times, then say the word "open" as you open it and take out the bubble wand. Say, "I blow bubbles," and then blow some bubbles. Say some short sentences, such as "Look at the big bubbles," "See lots of tiny bubbles," and "The bubbles popped!" The child will probably request a turn at

blowing. Hold the wand and show her how her mouth should look—exaggerate a scared face with a round mouth and pretend to blow. Some children may have difficulty executing this type of movement at this age. Encourage your child to request continuing by saying, "More? More bubbles? More bubbles!" and then continue to blow more. If your child has trouble puckering her lips to blow, she may become frustrated. To help her be more successful, cut a short length of a drinking straw and help her blow through the straw at the bubble wand.

8. **Pot of Stew.** Get a large metal pot and several favorite toys. Name each object as you pick it up. Say, "In the pot!" as you throw it in. Usually, the act of throwing an object and the sound of the object hitting the metal pot are fun for the child. Using a large spoon, pretend to stir the stew. Then dump the objects out of the pot.

9. **Animal Picnic.** Collect a few teddy bears or other stuffed animals and seat them around a small towel. Place some cups and spoons on the towel. Say, "We're having a picnic." As you place the cups, say, "We need cups. One for you, one for me, one for the rabbit, and one for the kitty. Let's have something to drink." Help your child place a cup to each animal's mouth and help the animal drink. Then say, "Let's have something to eat. We need some food." Use pretend objects or make food items out of Play-Doh. Narrate the activity with such expressions as "The animals are hungry. They want to eat." Then as you pretend to feed each animal, say, "Here you go, Rabbit! Here's *your* cookie. Do you want a cookie, Puppy?" and so on. Help your child attempt to feed one of the animals.

10. **Taking Care of Baby.** Using a large baby doll, enact several caretaking functions, modeling for the child and letting the child help. For example, say, "The baby wants her bottle. Let's feed the baby." Or, "The baby is going night-night [cover the baby with a small blanket]. Night-night, Baby!" Or, "The baby needs a bath! Let's wash her arms [legs/chest/tummy/face]."

Books to Buy or Borrow and Suggestions for Using Them

By now, the use and sharing of books is hopefully a regular part of the child's daily routine. The sturdy form-board books are still favorites, and now the child is beginning, with some help, to turn the pages and name the pictures. At this early stage, it is good to remember that just looking at a book together, using it as a basis for conversation, is an ideal language activity. It will help develop vocabulary and grammar and help increase knowledge about the world in general. It will also contribute to developing the child's attention span. The child is learning to associate reading with pleasure, an association that will help create a lifelong reader. By reading out loud, you are modeling the act of reading—something your child will want to imitate—and helping her become motivated to learn to read herself. Your local library can now become a major resource, since purchasing books can be expensive. Libraries often have special storybook-sharing times for the under-eighteen-month age range! To provide a complete list of appropriate books for this age would take up too much space, but here are some favorites recommended by librarians who specialize in early childhood:

Anno's Peekabook by Mitsumasa Anno

Trucks by Byron Barton

Hand Rhymes by Marc Brown

Baby's Good Morning Book by Kay Chorao

Pat-a-Cake and Other Play Rhymes by Joanna Cole and Stephanie Calmenson

Jack and Jill and Other Nursery Rhymes by Lucy Cousins

Tomie DePaola's Book of Poems by Tomie DePaola

In the Small, Small Pond by Denise Fleming

Babies by Rachel Isadora

I See by Rachel Isadora

All Fall Down (and Other Titles) by Helen Oxenbury

Have You Seen My Duckling? by Nancy Tafuri

Where Does the Brown Bear Go? by Nicki Weiss

Max's Bath (and Other Titles) by Rosemary Wells

A great time for book sharing is while the child is sitting in the high chair. Small sturdy form-board books are great for this, and some are even designed to be used with specific food such as Cheerios or raisins. For example, *The SunMaid Raisins Play Book* by Alison Weir has places on the page to place real raisins to be eaten as the book is interacted with. There is a similar book designed for Cheerios. Another favorite high-chair book is Richard Scarry's *Early Words*.

The books listed at the end of Chapter 1 are also still applicable for this age group. The number-one consideration in choosing a book is that the child enjoys it. Wherever possible, try to allow the child to do (or at least help with) the selection of the book. Remember, too, that a big part of the pleasure of reading comes from the physical closeness and one-on-one attention that the child is receiving. Pick places that are easy for cuddling positions, such as the corner of a couch or a bed. You can also create a special reading corner in the child's room, with a bookshelf, a special rug, a pillow, or a chair (beanbag chairs are great) and adequate lighting.

It's not too early to begin relating the books to real life, by connecting pictures in the book with objects and experiences the child is familiar with. For example, an extension of the book *Trucks* might be to collect the child's own toy trucks and have them nearby to talk about as the book is read. An extension of *Have You Seen My Duckling?* would be to take a small rubber or toy duck, hide it, and then go looking for it in various places.

Books with rhythm and rhyme are even more fun now. My son used to squeal with pleasure at being bounced on my lap as we read "Dum ditty dum ditty dum dum dum!" from *Hand, Hand, Fingers, Thumb* by Al Perkins. At the end of the book, he would say, "AGAIN!" It is common for children at this age to request repeated readings of a favorite book. This is an excellent situation for language acquisition. Have patience, and know that when you're on the third go of a favorite book, you're doing an important job!

Chapter 3

Age Two to Three: Learning How Words Go Together

The quickest way for a parent to get a child's attention is to sit down and look comfortable.

—Lan Olinghouse

It goes without saying that you should never have more children than you have car windows.

—Erma Bombeck

Once the child has mastered two-word combinations, three-word utterances begin to appear and to grow longer. "Mommy eat" and "Eat cookie" now become "Mommy eat cookie." At this age, the child is using approximately five hundred words and comprehending approximately nine hundred. The small "filler" words begin to appear that now make the child's speech sound more adultlike, though far from conventional.

Prepositions emerge, such as "in" and "on." Word endings, for example *-ing* and the plural *s* are used: "Mommy going" and "My cars." The acquisition of these forms has an amazingly predictable order, with *-ing* usually first, followed by "on" and "in." Next to appear is the use of the plural *s*, as in "cats," often misapplied and overgeneralized, as in "mans" or "mouses." Past-tense forms are used in the most common irregular forms (such as "got," "went") and with some regular *-ed* endings ("walked"). Once again, the rule is commonly overgeneralized as it is being acquired, so you may hear "comed" or "runned" as the child is in the process of learning the *-ed* ending. This is perfectly normal, and parents should refrain from overly correcting their child's grammar at this stage. Rather, it is better to simply repeat the child's utterance with the correct form so that the child can hear the correct model.

The use of *s* to indicate possession ("Mommy's car") and the third-person singular verb form ("Mommy goes") appears. Personal pronouns, such as "I," "me," "you," and "mine," usually are present by three years.

Early *wh-* question forms begin to be used, such as "What?" and "Where?" ("What you want?" "Where Daddy going?") It takes a while to get the word order correct, so you typically hear "Where that boy is?" before "Where is that boy?" Although the child may begin to use "Why?" she doesn't fully understand what that means. She may, however, realize that if she says "Why?" she gets people to talk more, as in the following example:

> It's time to put on your coat.
> Why?
> Because we have to go now.
> Why?
> Because it's getting late and Mommy has to go to work.
> Why?
> Because we have to pay the bills.
> Why?
> Because if we don't pay the bills then we'll have to move.

You get the point.

Helping verbs, such as "is" and "can," appear after about two and a half years of age, as do the articles "a" and "the." These are the filler words that enable the child's speech to start to sound more adultlike. So instead of the more telegraphic "I do it," you may hear "I can do it." Instead of "Kick ball," you may hear "Kick the ball." Instead of "The boy going," you'll hear "The boy is going."

It is this explosion in the acquisition of grammatical elements that makes some children seem so far ahead or behind their peers. This is a period of extreme variability in what is considered normal. Some two-year-olds have vocabularies of two thousand words, and there are three-year-olds with vocabularies of only a few hundred words. Considering that upon school entry, a child typically has more than six thousand words at her command, input at this stage takes on enormous importance.

Conversations Can Get Confusing

By three years, a child can participate in rudimentary conversations. However, these are much easier when they are pertaining to the here and now. The child tends to presume that listeners share his background knowledge, which can be cause for confusion. He might mention people or things listeners are unfamiliar with, assuming that they know all of the same things he does, as in:

> CHILD: I lost my robocat.
> ADULT: What's your robocat?
> CHILD: YOU KNOW! My ROBOCAT!

In terms of semantic development, the child now knows that "dog" does not refer to all animals, and has acquired the names of many animals. He can even begin to think categorically, that is, that objects can be sorted into categories, such as toys, animals, and foods. An excellent early-childhood game for this age is lotto, in which cards are drawn and placed on boards according to which category they belong to. By three the child has developed an understanding of many concepts, such as those of size ("big-little") and spatial relationships ("under," "over," "in front of," "behind").

The two- to three-year-old is continuing to develop in the area of play as well. Whereas at two, a child can combine two objects appropriately, as in combing a doll's hair or pretending to give a doll a drink from a cup or bottle, the three-year-old is now able to enlarge this into a sequence of actions, or a script. For example, the sequence of a nighttime routine, such as undressing, bathing, drying, putting on pajamas, getting into bed, and going to sleep, may be acted out on a doll. Other sequences, such as cooking and serving a meal, having a birthday party, going shopping, going to the doctor, and going to school, can be acted out as well.

Books involving these themes are excellent for this age. For example, stories where one character engages in a series of different actions, such as *The Very Hungry Caterpillar* or *Brown Bear, Brown Bear, What Do You See?* are excellent, as are books in which one location is explored—a trip to a zoo, pet store, or farm. These types of books help develop vocabulary organized around a unifying semantic category or theme. If you enjoy cooking, a simple project such as making a fruit salad can be fun.

It is helpful to remember that the child at this age thinks the world operates from his own perspective. Spending quality time with him will involve entering *his* world and interacting with objects and activities that he finds interesting. I found the following touching anecdote in *Parents* magazine, contributed by Mary Beth DeMartino from Frostburg, Maryland:

> My three-year-old son Sam came into the kitchen looking sad. When I asked why he wasn't watching TV with Daddy, he replied, "Daddy's watching the grass show again." I looked around the corner to see that my husband was watching a golf tournament.

Saying It Right

The acquisition of speech sounds is still a work in progress at this age. It is not uncommon for clustered consonants (for example, *sp, sl, st, fl, pl*) to be a problem. You may hear "dop" for "stop" or "feep" for "sleep." The formation of back and front consonants (*k* and *g, t* and *d*) may not yet be mastered, so these may be produced by the wrong end of the tongue, creating "doh" for "go," "tar" for "car," or "gawgie" for "doggie." Some long words may be pronounced in shorter form, with a syllable omitted, as in "puter" for "computer." One mom reported being taken aback by her preschool son at the beach one day. She usually brought along her binoculars so she could enjoy watching the sailboats out on the water. As she was unpacking and spreading the blanket, her son shouted, "Mom! You bring your 'knockers?'"

Ages and Stages

Word Order and Word Modifications

Two to Three Years

Receptive	Expressive	Motor
Points to pictures of objects	Three-word sentences develop	Imitates drawing O and +
Identifies objects from use ("Show me what we eat")	Asks *What* and *Where* questions	Stands on one foot briefly
Understands Q. forms *What* and *Where*	Makes negative statements: *Can't open it*	Builds tower of nine to ten blocks
Understands negatives: *no, not, can't, don't*		Likes to do things for self
		Beginning to match colors
		Beginning to establish handedness

Play Behavior

While truly cooperative play is not yet typically developed, children at this age begin to show imaginary pretend play, and enjoy being with other children. They can now reenact everyday events, such as shopping and going to the doctor, and can demonstrate some sense of sequence in their play, as for example, mixing, baking, and serving a cake or filling a truck with dirt and dumping out the dirt in another location.

Top Ten Activities for Children Two to Three Years of Age

1. **Photo Album.** Use a small ready-made photo album. Place pictures of family members, pets, friends, and favorite toys in the album. Also include pictures of the child doing several actions—eating, getting dressed, and so forth. Looking at the book together, ask and answer *Who* and *What* questions: "Who's that? That's Mommy. Mommy is in the car."

2. **Laundry Sort.** Have the child help you sort the clean laundry, naming the items and their owner. For example, "Here's a sock. Here's another sock. These are Sean's socks. Here are Mommy's socks. Here are Daddy's socks."

3. **Telephone.** Using toy telephones, pretend to call up your child. Enact a simple conversation, such as "Hi, Sean! How are you?" Make a comment and see if your child responds. If your child says, "Bye," and hangs up, then you hang up too. Then encourage the child to call you. You can expand the game by pretending to call another person, like Daddy or Grandma.

4. **Lotto.** This is an old tried-and-true favorite and one that is commercially available. (Ravensberger makes a nice version.) Place the cards facedown, and take turns drawing a card. Name the card together, then say to the child, "Who has a doll? I don't have a doll," or "I have a doll!"

5. **Shopping.** This can be adapted to many ages. Place several toy or real foods on a table. Ask the child to help you find a particular food and put it in a shopping bag. Take turns being the shopper, asking, "Do you have any _____?" Or you can each have a bag and take turns saying what you're taking: "I need some eggs," for example. Pretend to scan the price of each item as you place it in the bag. Use a toy cash register to complete the sale. Don't forget to say, "Have a nice day!" For a more challenging version, try a game that I call Shopping with Ernie. Place approximately twenty food items on a table. The child is the grocer. Ernie—or another *Sesame Street* character—is shopping and asks the child for three items to be placed in his bag. Have the child listen, then repeat the three items in order, then find them and place them in Ernie's bag.

6. **Story Tapes.** At this stage, the child usually has a few favorite books. It's fun to tape-record yourself reading and discussing these books with your child and then to let your child listen to the recording. Record each book on a separate tape, then place each book and its corresponding tape in a clear plastic food-storage bag. These can be hung in the child's book corner, along with a small tape recorder that the child is trained to use on his own when Mom or Dad is occupied. I developed a collection of these for my son and would use them in the car during our long daily commutes.

7. **Pizza Party.** Have a pretend pizza party. Invite several stuffed animals and seat them around a small table. Make a pizza using Play-Doh, and bake it in the "oven." Cut each guest a slice, then ask each animal, "Do you want pizza?" Role-play the animal's response: "This pizza is great!" or "I'm really stuffed" or "Can I have more pizza?"

8. **Zoo Trip.** Place several toy animals around the room in shoeboxes. Take a pretend stroll through the "zoo" (you can put a doll in a stroller or pretend the doll is walking too), and stop and look at each animal. You can pretend to feed the animals and talk to them.

9. **Birthday Party.** Have a birthday party for one of your child's dolls or stuffed animals. Using toy telephones, invite the guests—other dolls and animals. Bake a pretend Play-Doh cake and add pretend candles made out of small sticks. Sing the song and have the guest of honor make a wish and blow out the candles.

10. **Visit to the Doctor or Vet.** Pretend that one of the child's dolls or stuffed animals is sick. Make a pretend visit to the doctor or vet. This might involve calling to make the appointment, bringing the doll or animal to the doctor or vet, having the doctor or vet examine the patient and recommend treatment, going home, administering the treatment, and calling for a follow-up visit.

Books to Buy or Borrow and Suggestions for Using Them

The two- to three-year-old child delights in a wide variety of books and has begun to understand simple stories, such as *The Three Bears*. Popular books for this age group have a repetitive format centered around a character or theme. Typically, the character encounters or interacts with a series of related things. For example, in *The Very Hungry Caterpillar*, the caterpillar eats various foods; in *Ask Mr. Bear*, the boy asks various animals what he should get his mother for her birthday; and in *Sam Who Never Forgets*, Sam the zookeeper feeds each animal. Or there may be an experiential theme, such as in *The Snowy Day*, in which activities associated with snow are depicted. The following is a brief list of the many wonderful books that your child will enjoy. Also typical at this age is the child's tendency to want a particular book read over and over. This should not be discouraged, since it enables the child to soak up the vocabulary and sentence structures. Your local children's librarian is a great resource for helping your child pick out appropriate books. Be sure and attend your library's story hours!

> *Baby in the Box* by Frank Asch
> *The Three Bears* by Byron Barton
> *The Runaway Bunny* by Margaret Wise Brown
> *The Very Hungry Caterpillar (and others)* by Eric Carle
> *Jesse Bear, What Will You Wear?* by Nancy W. Carlstrom
> *Ask Mr. Bear* by Marjorie Flack
> *Corduroy* by Don Freeman
> *Happy Birthday!* by Robby H. Harris
> *The Snowy Day* by Ezra Jack Keats
> *Blueberries for Sal* by Robert McCloskey

Here Are My Hands by Bill Martin
Eat Your Dinner! by Virginia Miller
The Little Engine That Could by Watty Piper
Sam Who Never Forgets by Eve Rice
Caps for Sale by Esphyr Slobodkina
I Went Walking by Sue Williams

Use your imagination to create extension activities that correspond to these stories. I have a small collection of zoo animals, a miniature wagon, and a collection of tiny pretend foods that I use to reenact the feeding of each zoo animal as we read *Sam Who Never Forgets*. Children enjoy pretending to be Sam and talking to each animal or pretending to be the elephant who thinks Sam has forgotten to bring him food. *The Three Bears* is also fun to reenact by collecting small, medium, and large bowls, chairs, and beds and using a doll as Goldilocks. A toy train set up so that it has to go up an incline makes a great reenactment of *The Little Engine That Could*.

Photo: SW Productions / Brand X Pictures / Getty Images

Guidelines for Reading with Two- to Three-Year-Olds

Children of this age group generally don't like to sit still for very long and they like to be busy. For these reasons, you'll want to include books that:

- Have lots of engaging illustrations
- Center on a theme (for example, zoo animals, a farm, seasons)
- Are fun-sounding and rhythmic (for example, *The Foot Book*, nursery rhymes and poems)
- Repeat a phrase or sentence (*Brown Bear Brown Bear What Do You See?* or *The Gingerbread Man*)
- Allow participation: those with pop-up pictures, textures to feel, and so forth (*Wheels on the Bus, Pat the Bunny, Where's Kitty?*)

When reading the book:

- Allow the child to take the lead and respond to her comments by expanding on them
- Feel free to alter long sentences to make them simpler
- When reading repetitive books, stop and let the child fill in part of a phrase

If you would like further resources to help you with interactive reading techniques or with ideas for extension activities, check out *Read with Me* by Shari Robertson, or *Books Are for Talking Too!* by Jane L. Gebers. These are listed in Appendix B.

Keep on Singing

Many picture books lend themselves to being sung. For example, the pop-up version of *Wheels on the Bus* can be combined with singing the song. Other favorite songs at this age include "Old MacDonald Had a Farm," "If You're Happy and You Know It," "Muffin Man," "Down by the Station," "She'll Be Comin' Round the Mountain," "Head, Shoulders, Knees, and Toes," and "The Bear Went over the Mountain." Children of this age enjoy learning simple motor movements as they participate in songs. Rhythm band instruments can be purchased or created inexpensively. Use a spoon and pot for a drum, an empty container filled with rice or beans as a maraca, a strip of ribbon with bells sewn on, and—if you can stand the noise—two pot lids for cymbals.

Chapter 4

Age Three to Five: Learning to Have Conversations

Anyone who thinks the art of conversation is dead ought to tell a child to go to bed.
—Robert Gallagher

From the age of three to age five, children are learning to become social beings in the world at large and to use language to talk about events and experiences that are outside of the immediate context. They learn to talk about past events (where they went the day before and what they did), and future events (what they will be doing and where they will be going), as well as about abstract ideas, such as why things happen and value judgments.

Conceptually, they are increasing their understanding of words that express ideas of space ("next to," "in front of," "around"), time ("before," "after," "first," "last," "next," "daytime," "nighttime"), and quantity ("more," "least," "less," "a few," "many"). The understanding of these concepts is now reflected in the grammatical forms they use, such as the past tense, and in the joining of sentences together with such words as "then," "because," and "so." These sentences are far from the adult versions, however. It is not unusual for a four-year-old to tack *-ed* to indicate past tense onto words that normally don't require it (as in "we runned over there") or to confuse the cause with the effect (as in "he hurt his knee because he was crying").

Semantically, children are developing a solid sense that words are entities that can be grouped into categories, paired into opposites, or given definitions. At age three, they are still very much tied to the literal meaning and may not quite get the gist of an opposite's task. For example, one of the items in a commonly used test requires the child to fill in the missing opposite word. The responses of younger children can be humorous:

> EXAMINER: Ice is cold, fire is . . .
> CHILD: Hot.

EXAMINER: Good. Let's try another one: We're awake during the day,
             we sleep at . . .
CHILD: Grandma's house!

Children between the ages of three and five are also beginning to develop an awareness of the sound structure of words (more on that in the next chapter) and that words can begin with the same sound or rhyme with each other. Playing guessing games involving clues is a favorite activity and an excellent way to enhance these skills. The television show *Blues Clues* is very popular with this age group: The main character, with the help of his dog, Blue, finds clues that involve semantically related items, from which the answer is deduced. For example, the clues "rain," "clouds," and "thunder" will lead to the conclusion "thunderstorm."

Socially, children are learning to conform to more conventional behaviors. It is not uncommon for a three-year-old to protest, "But I don't WANT to do _____," as though that should be reason enough for not having to do it. Learning that you don't always get what you want or do what you want is a major accomplishment, and the four-year-old child who hasn't yet learned this principle will have a difficult time in the preschool classroom.

Three- and four-year-olds are learning to develop self-control with respect to directing their attention, resisting impulses, and handling anger. This growth process can be greatly assisted by the language used by their caregivers. For example, in a good nursery school or preschool classroom, you might hear a teacher helping a child form the words to express hurt feelings about what another child might have said, then prompting the second child to apologize, or helping a child to "use his words" to express anger about the action of another child.

Watching three-year-olds on their first day of nursery school can be fascinating as what might be termed "total chaos" gives way to order and routine. The patience and skills of a good teacher are a marvel to behold as she rounds up the group for their first circle time seated around her on the floor. Consider what the child must do: exercise self-control by sitting in one spot, directing and maintaining attention to either the teacher or another child who is having a turn at speaking, and controlling the many impulses that are occurring, such as talking out of turn, or playing with a child next to her.

Three-year-olds live their lives very much in the present. For this reason, it is usually fruitless to try to engage them in a conversation about anything other than what they are focused on at the moment. Ask a three-year-old a question while he's concentrating on something else, and he probably will just ignore the question. Children of this age group are beginning to appreciate the flow of time, that some things occur before others, and that there is an orderly progression of events. But don't ask them to concentrate on more than one thing at a time.

Owing to this developing sense of the flow of time, the ability to place picture cards in the correct sequence is emerging. As a rule of thumb, a three-year-old can generally place two or three pictures in order (once shown how); the four-year-old, four pictures; and the five-year-old, five or more. Picture-sequence stories and wordless books are an excellent activity for this age group, since they can be the basis for discussions of time concepts, such as "before" and "after," and, for the older child, of causal connections ("Why did the boy cry?" "Because he fell and hurt his knee") and inferences ("What do you think he wants to do now?")

By around age four, the developing understanding of internal feelings and reactions helps children become ready to comprehend stories whose characters respond emotionally to events and take actions that have consequences. The Curious George stories are beloved by four-year-olds because George typically finds himself, like they do, out of bounds in some way through no fault of his own, with some catastrophic event ensuing that causes great anger and commotion. And yet things usually turn out to be not only okay, but George winds up being a hero.

Four-year-olds tend to be quite literal, and unlike six-year-olds, who start to appreciate jokes based on double meanings, they will interpret words more concretely. This can result in some humorous, albeit embarrassing, moments, well represented in the beloved Dennis the Menace comic strip. For example, once Dennis asks the large-bellied Mr. Wilson, "Is it true what my dad says, that you can take a shower and not get your feet wet?" Another time Denis's dad is arriving home from work. With arms extended, Dennis excitedly ushers him into the house, saying, "I couldn't wait for you to get home, Dad. Mom said there would be plenty of fireworks when you got here!"

Humor for four-year-olds lies in incongruity and exaggeration. They especially love recounting ridiculously absurd situations. Try telling knock-knock jokes to three- to four-year-olds. They get the basic structural format, and they love saying the "knock-knock" part. But when you ask "Who's there?" what follows will be anybody's guess; they will typically make up some incongruous ending, roaring with laughter.

The child's ability to tell a story is also developing at this time. By age five, a child will have the ability to tell a story that has a recognizable beginning, middle, and end, with some sort of problem getting resolved. Four-year-olds may have some difficulty separating fantasy from reality in their recounting of real life events and they may exaggerate the truth or "make up tales" on occasion. They are not usually deliberately deceitful—for them there is not a clear line between what is real and what is imaginary, and they may need to be helped to learn the distinction. Their fears of monsters and scary creatures can be very real, and movies with particularly violent or frightening scenes may not be a good idea.

During this period, the child begins to learn polite forms—not just "please" and "thank you," but more polite ways of asking for things, refusing things, directing others, interrupting. When visiting, three-year-olds will look at a plate of cookies on the table and blurt out, "I want a cookie!" Four-year-olds, on the other hand, are apt to say, "Boy, I'm really hungry!" These more polite forms are what enable them to negotiate play successfully with their peers—sharing, waiting for turns, giving and following directions. From four to five years of age, much of the interaction between children takes place in the form of words. Research has shown that more verbally adept children tend to be more sought after as playmates, while the less verbal ones may tend to stay on the periphery of the interactions. A language-delayed three-year-old can get by just quietly playing alongside his peers, but by four, he will start to stand out. A well-attuned teacher can find ways to assist the child and make sure that he is included in play activities. She can also assist parents in selecting an appropriate child to invite to the home. Play dates are especially helpful for this type of child. It is much easier to participate when there is only one partner and no one else around to usurp the attention.

By around age five, owing to the acquisition of all of the aforementioned abilities, play takes on a much more complex and sophisticated quality. Entire sequences can be role-played by imaginary characters, with realistic problems, emotional reactions, and elaborate solutions. Opportunities for this type of dramatic play are important, which is why an overemphasis on, and too much direct teaching of, literacy skills at this age can be counterproductive. Aside from the issue of readiness for literacy skills, precious time for engaging in pretend play will be robbed from the child. Ironically, it is exactly the skills that are learned during dramatic imaginary play that form the foundation of reading comprehension: the ability to understand a character's emotions and motives, to make inferences based on given information, to attribute and invent dialogue, to create plots, and to resolve problems.

Saying It Right

The typical four- to five-year-old is a chatterbox, capable of extended conversations. He can discuss a multitude of subjects, remaining on a topic for several turns. By four years of age, the child should be completely intelligible, though not all sounds of the language will have been mastered. It is perfectly normal not to have mastered the *l* or *r* or *s* or *th* sound. However, the child should be fully understandable to those around him, including unfamiliar adults and peers. Of course, there may be an occasional mix-up when a particular word gets confused with another. One preschool girl was bragging that her mom had brought her new shoes from "Payweth." A peer said, "Pay-Less?" And the child, indignant, responded, "NO! PAYWITH!" The quick-thinking teacher remembered that the mother had a job that often took her to Europe and quickly interpreted that the girl was trying to say "Paris."

Ages and Stages

Three to Four Years

Receptive	Expressive	Motor
Begins to understand concepts of time (tomorrow), number (two), and comparison (bigger)	Uses complete sentences of three or more words	Preference for hand usage
	Speech is understandable to strangers, some sound errors may be present	Hops on one foot
		Draws a recognizable man
Can answer, "What do you do when you're _____ [sleepy]."	Has vocabulary of 1500 words	Imitates cross and square
		Completes eight-piece form-board puzzle
Understands "lets pretend"	Tells about past events	
Follows a two-stage command	Uses -*ed* at end of verbs	
	Repeats a nursery rhyme	
	Can sing a song	

Play Behavior

Cooperative play starts to emerge at this age, and children begin to share toys more readily. They will work together to reenact sequences, such as a birthday party. The language required for this level of play is more sophisticated. Words are needed in order to negotiate turns and reach agreements as to which objects will be used and who will assume various roles. Children are now more willing to wait for a turn.

Four to Five Years

Receptive	Expressive	Motor
Understands sequence of events (first, then, after)	Speech is fully intelligible	Draws a person with more details

Listens to long stories	Uses long, complex sentences joined by *then* and *and*	Colors a circle with some idea of staying within the lines
Follows complex directions	Can hold a conversation about past and future events	Imitates drawing of triangle
	Vocabulary of 2000 words or more	
	Can discuss causality, using *because* and *so*	

Play Behavior

By five years of age, children readily engage in imaginative play that involves organizing and planning more complex sequences of events. They enjoy using dolls and puppets to act out stories. They like projects that involve steps to complete, such as cutting and pasting. They are able to play well together in small groups of two to five children. Friendships become stronger and children will engage in fully cooperative play with peers of their choosing.

Top Ten Activities for Children Three to Four Years of Age

1. **Silly Faces.** This is a commercially available Colorforms set. Or you can use Mr. Potato Head. Take turns selecting each feature of the face until the face is completed. Then have the faces talk to each other, introducing themselves with made-up names and engage in pretend activities, such as having a snack or playing on the playground. This can be extended to drawing simple faces with markers. The child will enjoy talking about a "sad" face, an "angry" face, or a "scared face," as well as the traditional "happy" face.

2. **Sorting the Mail.** Collect pictures (or use commercially available category cards) depicting items from the following groups: food, clothing, toys, animals, and vehicles. Get five small boxes, one for each category. Mix up the pictures and place them facedown on a table. Sort the pictures: Pick them up one at a time, name them, and say the name of the category as each picture is placed in the appropriate box. For example, "What's this? It's a horse. A horse is an animal. The horse goes here."

3. **Go-togethers.** Collect or make picture-card pairs of objects that are related by use or function (for example, hammer and nails, bowl and spoon).

Turn the cards facedown on a table. Players keep drawing cards, turning them over and naming the object, until they get two that go together. They must explain how the two objects are related—"You hit nails with a hammer"—and then they get to keep the pair.

4. **Firehouse (Role Playing).** Collect items associated with firefighting, such as fire hats, oversized boots, yellow rain slickers, a small stepladder, a wagon, and a length of garden hose. Read *Fire!* by Joy Masoff. Visit a real firehouse (some have special open-house days for children). Create or purchase a set of picture cards depicting the sequence that typically takes place when there is a fire. Show children how to use the props, then let them play on their own. Another alternative is to use a toy firehouse with miniature fire trucks and firefighters. Children can create buildings with blocks and place toy people inside to be rescued. Paint or draw a picture of a fire truck. Make up a story about a fire. Discuss safety precautions in the home and what to do if there is a real fire.

5. **Doctor/Hospital (Role Playing).** Collect props, such as a white shirt for a lab coat and medical supplies, including Band-Aids, gauze, elastic braces, and cotton swabs. A doctor's kit can be purchased at most toy stores. An old pair of headphones can be adapted as a stethoscope. Set up a makeshift examination table using an ottoman, bench, or box covered with a white cloth or towel. A small rolling cart makes a great gurney. A toy phone can be used to arrange appointments. Shoe boxes and stuffed animals or dolls can serve as hospital beds and patients. Read a book about a doctor or hospital, then act out scenarios. Here are a few: *Curious George Goes to the Hospital* by Margret and H. A. Rey, *This Is a Hospital, Not a Zoo!* by Roberta Karim, and *Gaspard in the Hospital* by Anne Gutman.

6. **School (Thematic Play).** It's hard to find a child who doesn't enjoy playing school, especially one with older siblings who go off to that special place every day. The great thing about school props is that they are the same items you'll want to get your child to prepare him for reading and writing. Read *Timothy Goes to School* by Rosemary Wells. For a delightful wordless picture book, see *School* by Emily Arnold McCully. It's about a little mouse sibling who is too young for school but sneaks out when his mother isn't looking and ends up spending the morning in a classroom.

7. **Trip to the Ice Cream Shop/Fast Food Restaurant (Thematic Play).** Create tubs of various ice-cream flavors using Play-Doh (or real ice cream if you desire). Cones can be created out of sturdy paper, rolled into a cone shape, and stapled together. The server can wear an apron and cap, and will need a small scoop or spoon. Concepts such as "small," "medium," and "large," can be practiced, as well as "top," "middle," "bottom." Various toppings can be created separately and added as desired. A commercially available

Play-Doh set is available to simulate a fast-food restaurant. (See Appendix A for more ideas.)

8. **Draw a Person.** This activity can be made especially fun by using a cookie sheet with Jell-O or instant pudding powder spread on it or a baking pan with sand. (Sand can be wetted and packed down for better definition of lines.) Take turns making a large face with eyes, nose, mouth, ears, and hair. Though your three-year-old may not be ready to do this, you can add a line for the neck, a large circle for the body, and lines for arms, legs, fingers, and toes. This is also fun to do at the beach, using a sharp stick on wet sand, or in the bathtub, using shaving cream on the tile wall.

9. **Photo Album Show-and-Tell.** Gather your child's favorite toys or objects around the house. Take a picture of each toy or object. Place the photographs in a small photo album. Help your child narrate the album by talking about each object, describing the features of the object, telling why it's special and where it came from. Record the information on an audiotape for later playback. This activity can be modified to be a picture story about various family members or scenes from a special family vacation, trip, or outing. Gather appropriate photographs and place them in the album in sequential order. You can also make a small book by gluing the pictures on separate pieces of paper with dictated sentences written underneath and stapling the pieces of paper together. Then have the child illustrate the book and dictate the title. Help the child narrate the story, recording each page separately on a cassette recorder.

10. **Act It Out.** Read (or look at and discuss) a book that has a clear sequence of events, such as *Sam Who Never Forgets*, in which a zookeeper feeds the zoo animals various foods. Reenact the story using toy or stuffed animals and a toy person. Talk about what each animal wants to eat. A related activity is to take a series of photos of your child performing a sequence, such as getting ready for bed or making a sandwich. Place the photos in a photo album and help your child narrate the sequence. This activity is especially fun for family outings, such as trips to shows, events, and vacations.

Top Ten Activities for Children Four to Five Years of Age

1. **Hide-and-Tell.** This is like show-and-tell except that the object is hidden. The designated speaker selects an object and places it in a bag. He then gives clues to listener(s), who can ask questions and then guess what is in the bag. Prompt the child to give clues that include the object's function, where it is typically found, who typically uses it, and its size, shape, and other features.

2. **Name Game.** Pick a category. Take turns coming up with an item in that category. Continue until no one can think of another item. This activity can be done in the car, or it can be paired with a simple turn-taking game, such as Don't Spill the Beans or Don't Break the Ice. An easier version of this game would be to spread out picture cards from various categories on a table and to take turns locating and naming cards in a particular category.

3. **Fold-a-Story.** Using four to six pictures that depict a clear sequence, have the child tell the story, one picture at a time. (An excellent ready-made source is *Fold a Book,* by Monica Gustafson, available from Pro-Ed, listed in Appendix B.) Cut the pictures out and place them in a storybook made by folding a sheet of paper twice and stapling the bound edge. Help the child select the first picture for page one. Then have him find the picture of what happened next and so forth. Tape-record the entire story for replaying.

4. **Stick-Writing Story.** Take a long narrow strip of paper and fold it accordion-style to create a series of five or six panels. Beginning with the first panel, have the child come up with a main character that you or your child can draw on the panel. Create a series of events for this character, illustrating each panel as you go along. Let your imagination go wild! Let the child retell the story, using the pictures as a guide.

5. **Opposites.** There are commercially available games and card decks that depict opposites. Place a set of opposite cards face down on a table. Take turns flipping over the cards and naming the words. When an opposite pair is discovered, use the words in a sentence—for example, "At night it's dark; in the daytime it's light." Create an opposites book, with opposite words on facing pages.

6. **What Did You Say? A Barrier Game.** This requires two players, each seated on opposite sides of a barrier, such as a large game board turned on its side. Each player is given an identical set of blocks or Colorform shapes. One person is the speaker, the other the listener. The speaker directs the listener to complete the same design he is creating, one step at a time. The goal is to have identical designs when completed.

7. **Daily/Weekly Calendar.** This is a good age to begin a simplified personal calendar, which can be modular and magnetized on the back to stick easily to a refrigerator. Collect pictures (use drawings, photos, or cut out ones from magazines) depicting the activities of the day, such as eating breakfast, getting dressed, going to school, going to a friend's house, taking a nap, eating dinner, taking a bath, and going to bed. At the beginning of the day, the activities can be placed in a row in left-to-right order. At the end of the day, the events can be reviewed, using the past tense to tell

"what we did today." The next phase is to develop a calendar strip depicting each day of the week, with special events marked on appropriate days.

8. **Feelings.** Create a photo album of various emotions: happy, sad, worried, scared, sick, angry. Narrate an audiotape with your child, discussing situations or times that you have felt these emotions. You can create a picture book by helping your child draw a picture of each emotion. Help the child create sentences describing the emotions, such as "I felt sad when . . ." These can be compiled into a book for the child to reread at a later time.

9. **Guess My Name: A Category Game.** This is a wonderful way to pass the time when in a car or a waiting room. The speaker thinks of an item, names the category it's in, and gives two or three other clues about it. The listener must guess the item to get a turn to be the clue giver. This game can be made slightly easier by using small picture cards of items from various categories. Select five cards in each of the following categories: vehicles, animals, clothing, foods, and toys. Name each card as it is placed faceup in the appropriate row on a table. Take turns closing your eyes while the other person picks up a card and gives clues, starting with the category it belongs in. For example, "It's a food. You eat it for breakfast. You can put milk on it." Once the child gets a bit more sophisticated, she can simply give the clues without picking up the card. (Younger children, who will have an urge just to tell what the item is rather than to give clues, will need to actually pick up a card and hold it in front of them, physically hiding it from the partner.)

10. **Read and Retell a Favorite Book.** Use a book that involves a main character who resolves a problem. (Curious George books are great!) Talk about how the character felt and what you might do if you had a similar problem. Recall an event from real life that was similar and talk about how it was handled. Have the child retell the story, selecting an event from the beginning, the middle, and the end of the story. If the child is able, have him tape-record a sentence for each page. Children enjoy playing tapes back as they hear themselves "reading" the story.

Books to Buy or Borrow and Suggestions for Using Them

This is a rich and rewarding age period in which to be sharing books with your child. The child is now venturing out into the larger world and learning the social rules and expectations of situations outside the familiar experience of the immediate family—at school, for example, or at a friend's house. Children are learning about actions and consequences, discovering new rules and boundaries, developing self-control, and learning to separate reality from fantasy. It's no wonder there are many favorite books involving such themes as monsters, getting into trouble, dealing with frustration, losing control, and unexpected events. Reading and talking about their deepest fears and experiences helps children feel more in control, develop confidence, and build language skills, all at the same time.

Here are examples selected by children's librarians (the entire list broken down by age can be obtained at www.westchesterlibraries.org):

No Jumping on the Bed! by Tedd Arnold
Old Black Fly by Jim Aylesworth
Madeline by Ludwig Bemelmans
Sam and the Lucky Money by Karen Bhinn
Will I Have a Friend? by Miriam Cohen
Go Away, Big Green Monster by Ed Emberly
Millions of Cats by Wanda Gag
Roger Loses His Marbles by Susanna Gretz
Lilly's Purple Plastic Purse by Kevin Henkes
Bread and Jam for Francis by Russell Hoban
Chicken Little by Steven Kellogg
There's a Nightmare in My Closet by Mercer Mayer
If You Give a Mouse a Cookie by Laura J. Numeroff
The Tale of Peter Rabbit by Beatrix Potter
Curious George by H. A. Rey
Horton Hatches the Egg by Dr. Seuss
Ira Sleeps Over by Bernard Waber
Timothy Goes to School by Rosemary Wells
It Could Always Be Worse by Margot Zemach

These stories can act as a basis for lots of discussions that tap into what-ifs and whys. For example, a Curious George episode could be elaborated upon with further ways George might get into trouble. By using the actual story as a base, the child can come up with alternative details and events. Four-year-olds enjoy letting their imaginations run wild with all the possible ways one can get in trouble, since their own behavior is often out of bounds.

In addition to the rich conversations that may be had based on sharing the above books, it is possible to use books as the basis for setting up pretend-play scenarios. Similar to the story reenactment technique described in the previous section, the pretend-play extensions can use actual objects from a story for acting out and elaborating the ideas in the story. For example, *If You Give a*

Mouse a Cookie can be elaborated upon by creating other items that were not included in the story that the mouse might want to eat or use.

Guidelines for Reading With Three- to Five-Year-Olds

Keep an open agenda when reading the book. The child may want to interrupt and stop to chat here and there. Let the book serve as a basis for conversation and go with the flow. Try to include a variety of books, both fiction and nonfiction, that the child finds appealing. Use books that:

- Have a sequence of events that relate to one another (*Sam Who Never Forgets*)
- Have a definite story structure, such as setting, main character, a problem to be resolved, an attempt on the part of the main character to resolve the problem, and an outcome (*Three Little Pigs*)
- Stretch the imagination
- Relate to strong emotions, such as fear, anger, sadness (*Alexander and the Terrible Horrible No Good Very Bad Day*)
- Build the child's vocabulary
- Can be sung or chanted

When reading the book:

- Read the title and encourage the child to consider what the book will probably be about
- Mention the author and illustrator
- Encourage the child to stop and comment or ask you what a word means
- Wonder out loud "What might happen next?" or why an event occurred
- Personalize the story by considering what you would do if . . .
- Discuss and extend the topic ("We could make a gingerbread man . . .")
- Allow the child to "read" the book to you (tell the story using the pictures by himself) or pick an event from the beginning, middle, and end of the story; talk about what happened first, next, and last
- Follow up with a real-life experience related to the book (for example, take a trip to a real airport)

Songs, Chants, Rhymes and Finger Poems

This is a wonderful age for having fun with songs and finger poems. Using hands and fingers integrates the words with the movement of other muscles and provides a rich sensory-motor experience. Children love to move around, and these participatory language activities are great for them. Here are a few favorites:

"Five Little Pumpkins," "Ten Little Monkeys," "One Potato, Two Potato," and "Teddy Bear, Teddy Bear."

Nursery Rhymes Revisited

Nursery rhymes can now be learned and recited by the child. They are an excellent way to develop awareness of sounds and rhyming. Children will enjoy acting them out with finger puppets, props, or felt-board cutouts, especially "Humpty Dumpty," "Hickory Dickory Dock," "There Was an Old Woman," "Mary Had a Little Lamb," "Peter, Peter, Pumpkin Eater," and "Little Boy Blue."

Photo: Photodisc Collection / Photodisc Blue / Getty Images

Songs

So many great children's songs are available. Some old classics include "Hokey Pokey," "London Bridge Is Falling Down," "Ring Around the Rosy," "The Farmer in the Dell," "Old MacDonald Had a Farm," "There Was an Old Lady Who Swallowed a Fly," "This Old Man," "A-B-C Song," "This Is the Way," "The Bear Went Over the Mountain," and "The Itsy Bitsy Spider."

Books That Are Songs and Poems

Here are some books that combine singing or chanting with reading:

> *Old MacDonald Had a Farm* by Pam Adams
>
> *What a Wonderful World* by Ashley Bryan
>
> *Today Is Monday* by Eric Carle
>
> *Down by the Station* by Will Hillenbrand
>
> *Over in the Meadow* by John Langstaff
>
> *Who Took the Cookies from the Cookie Jar* by Bonnie Lass and Philemon Sturges
>
> *Hush Little Baby* by Sylvia Long
>
> *Chicken Soup with Rice* by Maurice Sendack
>
> *The Raffi Singable Songbook: A Collection of 51 Songs from Raffi's First Three Records for Young Children* by Raffi
>
> *Miss Mary Mack: A Hand-Clapping Rhyme* by Nadine Bernard Westcott
>
> *The Itsy Bitsy Spider* by Isa Trapani
>
> *Take Me Out to the Ballgame* by Jack Norworth
>
> *There Was an Old Lady Who Swallowed a Fly* by Simms Taback.

Chapter 5

Age Five to Six: Getting Ready to Become Literate

Every child is born a genius.
—R. Buckminster Fuller

The best thing to spend on your children is your time.
—Louise Hart

By age six, the child has basically mastered the spoken form of his native language. He can converse at length using long and grammatically complex sentences. Though fine-tuning of irregular verb forms is still occurring, the average six-year-old can solidly keep up his end of a conversation with an adult. He enjoys discussing a wide range of topics and loves to impress listeners with newly discovered bits of information about how things work and about the world in general. He is a virtual sponge, with a vocabulary that is continuing to grow, exploding to many thousands of words. For this reason, it is especially important that even though he may be learning to read himself, he will still enjoy having more difficult books read to him. He will acquire lots of vocabulary through this activity, as well as through conversations around him, television, movies, and books he reads himself.

Once children have mastered speaking their language, they are ready to begin thinking about words as separate entities that can be analyzed and talked about. Educators refer to this as metalinguistics (being able to talk about talking). For example, children begin to notice that words can start with the same sound; can rhyme; can be short, made up of only a few letters, or long, with lots of letters; can have beginning, middle, and ending sounds; and can be broken down into smaller parts or can go together to form things called sentences. They notice that some sentences are questions and that they usually begin with the words "what" "where," "who," "when," or "why." It is at this point that children are showing the readiness to begin learning to read and write. While they may have already learned to recite the alphabet correctly, they are now developing the idea that the letters correspond to the sounds in the words we speak. They usually become interested in learning to form letters and to learn letter sounds, and enjoy writing their names, their friends' names, and several basic words. They can recognize many brand-name labels, and some children may even be reading. They are now ready to hold a pencil or crayon the proper way and to copy more complicated shapes and patterns.

By this age, children have grasped that a word can have two different meanings, so they start to appreciate word-play humor and jokes, such as "Why does a spider make a great baseball player?" *(They're good at catching flies)* and "What has three eyes but can't see?" *(Mississippi)*.

While some children are already reading at this age, it is important to recognize this phase of phonemic-awareness development and not to rush them into reading before they are ready. Children may begin to recognize many words by sight and even to "read" (more likely memorize) a favorite storybook, but in order to become a truly successful reader, it is essential that they acquire knowledge about the relationship of letters to sounds and about the sound patterns of words. It is common for children to begin the reading process by pretending to read, but this eventually gives way to actually decoding the words once children have acquired knowledge of the sounds associated with the letters. In fact, research on children with dyslexia (a reading disability) has shown that an understanding of sound categories and the underlying sound patterns that letters represent is a primary area of weakness for such students. (See Chapter 11.) If a child is urged or forced to read before she has acquired the necessary readiness to do so, she may come to overly rely on memorizing the words solely based on their visual pattern. While this strategy will work for a while, the child's memory quickly becomes overloaded with trying to remember words this way, and reading will not progress in the way that will lead to success. (See Chapter 10.)

Ages and Stages

Five to Six Years

Receptive	Expressive	Motor
Comprehension of vocabulary builds to approximately 13,000 words by age six (doubles between the ages of six to seven)	Communicates well with family, friends, or strangers	Begins to learn how to write and form letters
	Gives and receives information easily	Copies rectangle with diagonal lines inside

Demonstrates preacademic skills ("metalinguistic" awareness) such as phonemic segmentation

Can take appropriate turns in lengthy conversations

Continues to fine-tune grammar (irregular verb forms such as *put*)

Can copy a diamond shape

Builds elaborate constructions with blocks

Play Behavior

Cooperative play has already been fully developed. Imaginary play includes complex scenarios with elaborate dialogue and role playing. Children are now capable of more elaborate types of organized group activities, as well as playing games and being involved in projects that involve more complicated rules and procedures.

Top Ten Activities for Children Five to Six Years of Age

1. **Memory Stretchers.** Here's an old favorite. One person starts out by saying, "I'm going to Grandma's house, and I'm going to pack . . . [pajamas]." The next person must repeat the first person's sentence and add one item: "I'm going to Grandma's house, and I'm going to pack my pajamas and my toothbrush." And so on. Other starter sentences are "I'm going shopping, and I'm going to buy . . ." "I'm writing a letter to Santa, and I'm asking him for a . . ." and "I went to the zoo, and I saw a . . ."
2. **Rhyme Time.** One person thinks of a short word, such as "hat." The next person must come up with a word that rhymes—for example, "bat." The third person must come up with yet another rhyming word. The game continues until no one can think of a new item that hasn't already been named. A more involved version of this game is to create a set of cards or objects, and a corresponding set consisting of their rhyming mates. Place one set on a table. Give the child a card or object from the second set and have him find its corresponding rhyming mate. Here are some suggested rhyming words: boat-goat-coat, rug-mug-bug, fish-dish, parrot-carrot, chair-bear, moon-spoon, bell-shell, hook-book, sock-rock, and fox-box.
3. **Beginning Sound Games and Chants.** Here are several variants:

    *   Same as above rhyming game, but instead of rhyming, the next word must have the same beginning sound.
    *   Object sorting: A fun project is to collect a set of tins or plastic containers. Label each with an alphabet letter (uppercase and lowercase). Collect objects that begin with each of the letter sounds, and sort them into the cans in which they belong.

- "*A*" My Name Is Alice: Teach the old jump-rope chant, which can also be done while bouncing a ball. The chant goes like this:

  > "*A*" my name is [say a name beginning with the letter A]
  > And my husband's [or wife's] name is A_____.
  > We come from A_____,
  > And we sell a_____s.

  Continue with the letter *B*, then *C*, and so forth, until the entire alphabet has been recited.

4. **Barrier Games.** These were mentioned in the Top Ten Activities for Children Four to Five Years of Age but are also excellent for this age. Some commercially available games, such as Guess Who? are very suitable. Each player has an identical array of pictures, in this case, people. The speaker must give clues so that the listener can identify the character being described—for example, "It's a woman. She has blond hair and earrings." Or players can take turns asking questions: "Is your person a woman?"

5. **Similarities and Differences.** By age five or six, children should be able to begin thinking about abstract features of objects and to compare their various features. A natural way to encourage this is to help your child start some kind of collection: rocks, bottle caps, shells, bugs. It can be fun to discuss and compare features—size, color, texture, and function—as a new item is introduced to the collection. Here is a game to help develop descriptive language: Create a set of cards of various items to be described. Have each player select a card. Give a token (a penny or a poker chip) to a player for every feature he can think of to describe his object. Examples of features for a banana may include "It's a food," "It's a fruit," "It's yellow," and "You peel it."

6. **Go Fish.** This is a great first card game for children this age. All you need is a set of cards containing pairs of items. These can be alphabet letters, solid-colored cards, shapes, or colored pictures that differ by only one feature (for example, an orange bear with blue skates versus an orange bear with red skates). General categories can be used as well, in which two animals, for example, would constitute a pair, and players would ask, "Do you have any animals?"

7. **Plan-Do-Tell Activities.** These can include such events as a party, a shopping trip, and a sightseeing excursion. The idea is to include the child in some written form of planning, involving list-making (grocery list, party guest list, list of places to visit). Take photographs of the planning process and then of the actual event itself. Place the pictures in a photo album, and record the events on an audiotape.

8. **Alphabet/Letter-Sound Games.** Here are a few versions to try:

    - *Alphabet Song:* Write all the alphabet letters in uppercase on a long strip of paper. Have the child sing the song as each letter is touched.
    - *Letter Find:* Place letter tiles facedown and give each player an alphabet-letter strip. Take turns picking up a letter tile and placing it next to the correct letter on the strip as the letter is named.
    - *The Name Game:* Give each person a paper strip with his or her name written in uppercase letters. Take turns drawing letter tiles. If the letter a player draws appears in his or her name, the tile is placed on the name strip. Keep playing until all the names are completed.
    - *Can It:* Collect small coffee cans. Paint or cover them with fabric and place an alphabet letter on each can. Have the children collect and sort small objects into the cans, based on the first sound of the word; for example, in the *B* can might be a bow, a ball, a baby, a bottle, and a bear.
    - *Alphabet Soup I:* Put a set of letter tiles in a small bowl. Assign each person a short word such as "cat" or "dog," and write it in uppercase letters on a card. Using a spoon, take turns drawing letter tiles until each word is completed.
    - *Alphabet Soup II:* Give each player a bowl. Take turns picking up letter tiles out of a pot. Once the letter and/or letter sound is named, the tile can go into that player's bowl.
    - *Alphabet Soup III:* Retrieve a letter tile from the bowl. Have the child name the letter, the sound it makes, and a word that begins with that sound in order to keep the letter.

9. **Invented Spelling or Writing Activities.** These are informal play situations in which writing is involved. The child is provided a paper and pencil and encouraged to act out various situations: taking an order in a restaurant, selling raffle tickets, making a grocery list or a list of ingredients for a cooking project, writing down the names of animals in an imaginary zoo, labeling stuffed animals with their names, having a pretend store and putting pretend price tags on items, creating a phone book or menu, writing a secret message, or making a guest list for a party.

10. **Who Did What, Where, When?** Create four baskets or small boxes containing picture cards that answer each of the above words (that is, a set of persons, actions, objects, locations, times). Try to include actions that can be performed on objects, for example, "kick," "throw." Pick one card from each basket, and try to make a sentence, even if it sounds silly. An alternate game is to place all the cards facedown. A player must choose a card and generate a question to which the card provides the answer. For

example, if someone picks a picture of a policeman, the question might be "Who helps you when you get lost?"

Books to Buy or Borrow and Suggestions for Using Them

Some children will have begun reading by this time, but it is important to still continue to read out loud to them. Reading books out loud will continue to develop their vocabulary and sense of story plot and characters. Make sure to include nonfiction books in areas of interest to them. For example, there is a book for just about any career that sparks their curiosity. Here are a few listed by Esme Raji Codell in *How to Get Your Child to Love Reading:*

Construction worker: *Joe and the Skyscraper* by Dietrich Neumann
Firefighter: *Fire!* by Joy Masoff
Police Officer: *Officer Buckle and Gloria* by Peggy Rathmann
Veterinarian: *One Day at Wood Green Animal Shelter* by Patricia Casey

Similarly, there is a book for just about any occasion that is big in the life of a five- to six-year-old. Here are a few listed by Codell:

Losing teeth:	*The Story of the Tooth Fairy* by Tom Paxton
	The Lost Tooth Club by Arden Johnson
	The Real Tooth Fairy by Marilyn Kaye
	Throw Your Tooth on the Roof: Tooth Traditions from Around the World by Selby B. Beeler
Birthdays:	*It's My Birthday!* by Pat Hutchins
	Happy Birthday to You! by Dr. Seuss
	Benjamin's 365 Birthdays by Judi Barrett
	How Many Candles? by Helen V. Griffith
	Lyle and the Birthday Party by Bernard Waber
Sleeping Over:	*Ira Sleeps Over* by Bernard Waber
	Rabbit's Pajama Party by Stuart J. Murphy
	Overnight by Adele Griffin
	Porcupine's Pajama Party by Doug Cushman
Naughtiness:	*Bootsie Barker Bites* by Barbara Bottner
	The Tale of Peter Rabbit by Beatrix Potter
	The Temper Tantrum Book by Edna Mitchell Preston
	The Rotten Ralph series by Jack Gantos

There are plenty of alphabet and counting books, as any visit to the local library or bookstore will reveal. Two particularly enjoyable ones are *What Pete Ate from A to Z* by Maira Kalman and *Six Dogs, 23 Cats, 45 Mice, and 116 Spiders* by Mary Chalmers.

Books containing silly jokes and riddles accentuate the child's newfound ability to appreciate words with double meanings. The Amelia Bedelia series is a hoot. Amelia, the housekeeper, creates havoc as she literally follows various instructions, such as "draw the drapes." Wordless picture books are a great way for children at this age to feel as though they are becoming independent readers, even if they are not yet decoding written words. For a list of wordless books, see Chapter 10. Another great way to pave the way from spoken language to reading is to have your child dictate his own story to you. (See Chapter 10 for ways to make homemade books.) Finally, there are some books children can start to read on their own after reading them with you several times. The secret to the success of these books is that the words are highly predictable due to their repetitious structures. Esme Codell highly recommends the All Aboard Reading series published by Grosset and Dunlap. The easiest level, Pictured Readers, includes *Space Kids* by Roberta Edwards, *Benny's Big Bubble* by Jane O'Connor, *Pig Out!* by Portia Aborio, *Silly Willy* by Maryann Cocca-Leffler, and *Don't Wake the Baby!* by Wendy Cheyette Lewison. Another series, published by Candlewick Press, consists of eight-page books, such as *Monkey Trouble* by David Martin and *Well Done, Worm!* by Kathy Caple.

Also check out children's magazines, such as *Ladybug, Cricket, Spider, Your Big Backyard,* and *Creative Kids Magazine,* in addition to the usual fare, *National Geographic Kids* and *Nick Jr. Family Magazine.*

There are several web sites that make books and stories available online. (See "Visit a Virtual Library: Web Sites With Online Books for Kids" in Appendix B.)

Books to Help Parents

If you want some more detailed tips on how and what to read with your child, you will probably enjoy the following books. Both are great resources and well worth the investment:

> *The Read-Aloud Handbook* by Jim Trelease
> *How to Get Your Child to Love Reading* by Esme Raji Codell

Songs and Chants

Now that more fine-motor maturation has taken place, many children, especially girls, enjoy hand-clapping songs, such as "Miss Mary Mack." You can get the book version by Nadine Bernard Westcott. Other chantable books include *There Once Was a Man Named Michael Finnegan* by Mary Ann Hoberman, *Little Rabbit Foo Foo* by Michael Rosen, and *Mary Wore Her Red Dress and Henry Wore His Green Sneakers* by Merle Peek. For a list of more books that can be sung and/or chanted, see the end of Chapter 4.

Summary of Part 1

- The development of spoken language is an amazing accomplishment that will form the basis of learning to read and write and will help determine success in school and beyond.
- Input matters: Language is developed through specific interactions, which will vary according to age:

0-1 year:	Communicate frequently; keep input short, simple, child-directed; be responsive.
1-3 years:	Allow the child time to initiate, build on the child's utterances, speak slowly and clearly.
3-5 years:	Develop conversational skills through discussions, encourage sociodramatic play.
5-6 years:	Develop awareness of the structure of language through word and sound games.

Self-Check 2: Take a Sample of You and Your Child Talking

Gather together the following objects: a small set of blocks, a tub of Play-Doh, some paper, and several markers or crayons. Using a cassette tape recorder or video camcorder, record a ten-minute segment of you and your child conversing (just the two of you) as you interact freely with the objects. Choose a quiet location, free of interruptions. Transcribe part (or all, if you wish) of the tape using the following format:

Your Utterances	Child's Utterances

Part 2

Talking Together

Introduction

Styles and Personalities

One of the major ways we as humans convey our personality is through language. Styles vary from culture to culture, within cultures, among individuals, and within individuals, depending on the task or situation. Deborah Tannen has written several books on cultural and gender variation in language style among adults. She analyzed a dinner-party conversation among a group of friends, which included people from New York, California and England. The New Yorkers' style was fast-paced, with frequent overlaps—that is, just before one speaker had completed a sentence, the speaker from New York was already initiating a turn. Others tended to wait for a complete pause before beginning to speak. Afterward, some felt that the New Yorkers had dominated the conversation. One could imagine them on the way home saying, "Those New Yorkers were so rude! Always interrupting! I couldn't get a word in edgewise!" Meanwhile, the New Yorkers were of the impression that the others had been reticent and standoffish. What had really occurred was a cultural mismatch in the participants' perception of the conversation that involved overlap time. Among mutually familiar speakers of some groups, overlaps can be a sign of "high involvement," according to Tannen. However, for those used to longer pauses between speaking turns, such overlaps are perceived as interruptions. In some Native American cultures, children are expected to be quiet when an adult is teaching—a style that can conflict with, and be misinterpreted by, mainstream American teachers. These are just a few examples of ways in which cultures may differ in their speaking habits. Knowledge of these cultural influences is important for classroom teachers, who may have different expectations about children's conversational styles.

In addition to the variation in styles of conversation based on cultural differences, there are also differences in personality that must be considered.

Different personality types or styles will manifest variation in language behaviors. The following are four styles that have been identified:

- **The Social, Outgoing Child.** This is the child who is friendly and quick to approach peers and adults, always ready to initiate conversational interaction. He is usually very tuned in to the emotional side of friends and quick to pick up on the moods of others. He is highly verbal and loves being in the center of the action.
- **The Quiet, Shy Child.** This is the child who prefers to remain on the periphery of a group and observe rather than jump right in. This child might need some time to become comfortable before being expected to say an awful lot. He may require drawing out on the part of a patient, caring teacher. He has a tendency to become invisible in very large groups and may need opportunities created by the teacher to have speaking floor time.
- **The Independent Child.** There's usually at least one in every group! This child has a mind of his own, knows exactly what he wants or doesn't want, and is quick to let you know when something isn't on his agenda at a particular moment! He needs plenty of opportunities for making his own decisions and can be a challenge, but he can also be an excellent leader.
- **The Follower.** This is the child who is more comfortable being a responder and may not always give a lot of responses, will tend to imitate others (often the very ones you wish he wouldn't) and can be easily dominated by stronger personalities. He may need some help learning to make up his own mind and that it is okay to disagree with others.

Within the framework of these four styles, we assume that the types of interactions we have with children will vary according to the child's personality, because part of what determines an interaction is the other person.

Chapter 6

Conversational Strategies: Three EX-s and a Whale

The words that a father speaks to his children in the privacy of home are not heard by the world, but, as in whispering-galleries, they are clearly heard at the end and by posterity.

—Jean Paul Richter

Why, a four-year-old child could understand this report. Run out and find me a four-year-old child.

—Groucho Marx

There are various ways to help make children feel comfortable and more likely to converse. Many are obvious but bear stating anyway. Most can be found in books and commercially available materials dealing with ways adults can best interact with young children in order to encourage the development of language. Two excellent and readily available programs upon which this chapter is based are the Good Talking With You videotape series of training programs available from Educational Productions, and *Learning Language and Loving It*, available from Hanen. The following are some basic suggestions to keep in mind.

Be on the Level

Picture yourself trying to have a conversation with someone twice your height. (Think about it—some giant about twelve feet tall.) How would you feel? Very small! Try to have the height of your head match that of your child's. For example, if you are sitting in a regular chair, place the child in a high chair or booster seat. Or sit down on the floor with your child.

See Eye to Eye

This is a basic principle of all good communication, but it is especially important with children. Remember, you're also modeling what you want your child to be learning to do. If you're having a conversation while you're driving, that's one thing, but at home, sometimes we adults have so many things to do that we talk while we're busy with something else. Some children have a strong habit of not engaging in eye contact. With such a child, you may need to get his attention and then wait, showing that you expect him to look at you (you might even have to ask) and then speak.

Be Here Now

When you make a comment or ask a question, have it pertain to whatever the child happens to be concentrating on at the moment. This will make your words more relevant to the child, and the child in turn will be more likely to respond, which is more important for younger children (ages 0-3), because the present moment is what they are capable of talking about primarily at this age.

Strategy 1: EX-plain—Label and/or Describe

Labeling and/or describing is exactly what that name implies: The adult labels and/or describes what the child is doing or looking at. The adult serves as the narrator of the ongoing scene. *No response is required on the child's part.* While this seems simple, it can be difficult for those who are used to overusing questions as a way of interacting with children. For example, if a child is playing with blocks, you might say, "You put the red block on top. Now you're putting on the green one. The tower is getting higher and higher." Or while bathing your child you might say, "I'm putting the soap on your arm. Now I'm washing your neck and your shoulders." Or while watching your child play you might say, "The bulldozer is pushing the dirt. It's going into a big pile." Most children enjoy this type of attention focused on them. There is no pressure to respond, and they are hearing many words and ideas that are connected to their immediate experience.

    This technique is helpful with shy children or with children that you haven't met before. Adults may feel awkward trying this technique at first, because it is not typical of the way adults talk to one another. A key factor is to remain focused on the child's actions and eye gaze. Since the child is primarily focused on the sensory experience, you should keep the content simple and concrete, using words that describe the quantity or quality of the objects involved.

Try the technique with another adult. One person will role-play the child; the other will role-play the adult. Tape-record what is being said and then transcribe it on paper. Remember, NO QUESTIONS!

Strategy 2: EX-pand—Make It Longer and More Complete

Expansions are responses to a child's utterances. The adult takes the child's word or words and expands them in some way (for example, adds a word or two). Unlike labels or descriptions, expansions require that the child say something, which may mean that the adult has to WAIT until the child does. The adult's expansion is a way of acknowledging the child's utterance and responding directly to it. In this way, the child knows she has been heard and understood, her attempt to communicate has been supported, and more information has been added. This new information could be in the form of adding a grammatical feature:

> CHILD: Go car.
> ADULT: Yes, we're going in the car.

Or the new information could be in the form of a vocabulary word or concept:

> CHILD: Car going.
> ADULT: The car is going under the bridge.

Expansions can also be more elaborate and extend the meaning and topic:

> CHILD: Cookie fall down.
> ADULT: Yes, the cookie fell on the floor. Now we can't eat it. It's dirty.

Or:

> CHILD: Go car.
> ADULT: Yes, we're going in the car. We're going to see Grandma.

Expansions enable conversations to keep going. They depend on the adult's ability to hear and understand the *child's* words and then to add information that is of *interest to the child*. Here are some contrasting examples:

Attuned Adult	Not Attuned
CHILD: Cup.	CHILD: Cup.
ADULT: You found a cup. The cup is empty.	ADULT: What's that doing here? That goes in the kitchen.

CHILD:	New ball.	CHILD:	New ball.
ADULT:	You have a new ball.	ADULT:	Oh, you got a new ball.
	I'll bet you can bounce		That's great.
	that ball really high.		

In each of the above cases, the attuned, child-centered responses would be more enabling for the child to continue the conversation, whereas the other examples would not.

Try some expansions. The following are some utterances spoken by a child. Write down your expansion next to each utterance.

My brother coming.   _____

_____

Truck over there.   _____

_____

No more juice.   _____

_____

Strategy 3: EX-tend—Keep the Conversation Going

Extending keeps the conversation going and continues the topic under discussion. In an example given in the preceding section, the child said, "Cookie fall down." After the adult expanded the sentence to "Yes, the cookie fell on the floor," the adult went on to extend the topic by talking about not being able to eat the cookie because it was dirty. Extensions link the idea at hand to something closely related. They allow conversations to continue over several turns, covering a range of topics that are linked by an idea. Here are more examples of extensions:

CHILD:	Go car.
ADULT:	Yes, we're going in the car.
	Where are we going? [Extension]
	Are we going to Grandma's house?
CHILD:	Go car Gamma's house.

Or:

CHILD:	Boots?
ADULT:	Yes we have to wear our boots. [Expansion]
	It's cold outside. [Extension]

Use the WHALE Principle

- **W = Watch** what your child is doing and attending to and try to figure out what she might be thinking about.
- **H = Hear** what your child is trying to say, whether it is just the babbling of a six-month-old, a grunt while struggling to reach for something, or a word or phrase.
- **A = Adjust** your own intentions or goals of the moment and join your child in whatever he is focusing on.
- **L = Listen** for a good opportunity to take a turn talking; you may have to endure some silent pauses, but wait for the child to initiate.
- **E = Extend** the interaction by responding to the child's utterance in an open-ended way.

Researchers in child language call this contingent responding, that is, responding to the child's attempt to communicate by saying something that relates directly to what the child has said. Contingent responding has been shown to be a powerful factor in language acquisition. Studies of infants have reported a strong correlation between the amount of contingent responding by mothers and the rate of language acquisition of their infants. Now, while language acquisition is not a race, and just because one child speaks earlier than another does not mean that the later-speaking child will have difficulties, it is interesting to note that contingent responding does, in fact, help the process along.

Do	Don't
• Wait for the child to speak	• Dominate the conversation
• Be attentive	• Divide your attention by doing something else you need to get done
• View the conversation from the child's perspective	
• Make questions open-ended	• Ask too many questions
• Add to the child's comments	• Demand a response
• Keep the topic going	• Have a strong agenda
	• Judge the child's utterances in terms of correctness of grammar

Chapter 7

So Glad You Asked: Asking Good Questions

Children ask better questions than adults. "May I have a cookie?" "Why is the sky blue?" and "What does a cow say?" are far more likely to elicit a cheerful response than "Where's your manuscript?" "Why haven't you called?" and "Who's your lawyer?"
—Fran Lebowitz

The parents exist to teach the child, but also they must learn what the child has to teach them; and the child has a very great deal to teach them.
—Arnold Bennett

Up to this point the use of questions has not been dealt with and, in fact, has been discouraged when applying the strategy of labeling and/or describing, explained in the preceding chapter. But questions are an important part of conversation and certainly play a big role in classroom talk, as we'll discuss in the next section.

Photo: Ryan McVay / Photodisc Red / Getty Images

Interrogator Versus Conversational Partner

Before discussing the types and levels of questions, it is useful to keep the following in mind. I like to make an important distinction between the terms "interlocutor" and "interrogator." "Interlocutor" literally means "in between the words"—in other words, getting inside what the other person wants to say and helping to draw that person out. It implies the joint cooperation of two or more people to share words and meanings. "Interrogator," on the other hand, conjures up images of interrogation rooms with bare lightbulbs and a less than appealing conversational partner grilling someone for a desired answer. I guess it's obvious which is preferable when dealing with children and which they would prefer. When communicating with a less capable partner, we often resort to questions as a way to get the person to talk more. But there is an art to this, as anyone who has watched a really good interviewer knows. The trick is to phrase the question in such a way as to spur the other person on. In the videotape series Good Talking With You, one video is titled *Now You're Talking: Techniques that Extend Conversations*. This videotape provides excellent examples of how to use questions in a nondirective manner. The following are examples of direct questions:

> What is that? A ball.
> What color is it? Blue.
> Is it yours? Yes.

Notice how these direct, interrogation-type questions are not only somewhat dominating, but they also stop the conversation. In contrast, indirect or more open-ended questions help spur further conversation. The following are examples of open-ended questions:

> I wonder what will happen next.
> Why do you suppose he's sad?
> If you were that boy, what would you do?

In contrast to direct questions, indirect, or open-ended questions have a number of attributes. Some of these are listed in the video's facilitator's guide, written by Carrie Sharp. Indirect, or open-ended questions

- Don't demand a response
- Don't have right or wrong answers
- Encourage thinking and problem solving
- Stimulate the use of imagination
- Send a message that the child's ideas are of value

The same guide lists some examples of indirect question and/or starter phrases:

- What would happen if . . .
- I wonder . . .
- What do you suppose . . .
- How did that happen?
- What do you think?
- Tell me about . . .
- What would you do?

- How can we . . .
- How did you . . .

Once you get used to using indirect questions, you'll find them to be a very effective means of eliciting conversation. Other attributes of indirect questions mentioned in the guide are that they

- Can sometimes begin with a comment, followed up with a request for further information, and can encourage children to recall their actions and experiences ("That's a great spaceship. Tell me how you made it.")
- Can be used to facilitate play sequences ("I wonder where that horse will go now.")
- Are appropriate in many types of activities
- Can be used to teach problem solving ("Tell me what you are trying to do. What else could you try?")
- Encourage children to be more specific in their choice of words ("Fixed it? What do you mean? Tell me more.")

That's a Tough Question: Easier and Harder Questions

Marion Blank, a well-known author of books, tests, and materials dealing with preschool language development, devised a way of categorizing questions into four distinct levels of complexity. For purposes of simplicity, I have collapsed these into three. The general idea of Blank's levels is that the closer the question relates to the immediate perceptual reality of the child, the easier it is for the child to answer it. If the answer to the question is right in front of the child and all she has to do is look at it and label it, that is easier than having to reason or make a judgment about an idea that is not obvious from a picture or situation.

Questions-Levels of Complexity

Different forms of questions entail various types of thinking and levels of difficulty. Here is a simple breakdown:

Level 1: Yes/No and Choice Questions
Is that a boy or a girl?
Are you eating lunch?
Do you want blue or red?

It's easy to see why these are the easiest: They require only a yes or no response from the child or provide a choice of answers. These questions are often used by teachers as a strategy to guide a child to the correct answer after she has given an incorrect response. For example:

TEACHER:	Joey, which color paint do you want to use?
JOEY:	[Looks at the paint, pauses, looks at the teacher, and hesitates.]
TEACHER:	[Holds up two jars of paint.] Do you want BLUE? Or RED?
	[Holds up each jar in turn as she says the colors.]
JOEY:	[Points to the blue one.]
TEACHER:	You want the blue one. You can say, "I want the blue one."

Level 2: Simple *Wh*-Questions/Product Questions
What's that?
What is the boy holding?
What do you do with a fork?
Where is the cake?
Who is looking in the window?

Such questions are slightly more difficult, since they require some specific knowledge (or product) to be provided. However, they are helpful in directing a child's attention. Parents use them a lot when looking at picture books with younger children. One- to two-year-olds quickly learn to ask "What's that?" as a way of getting information while enjoying shared picture-book reading. These questions can also be used to guide a child to a correct answer:

TEACHER:	What do you think is going to happen?
CHILD:	I don't know.
TEACHER:	What is the boy carrying?
CHILD:	His kite.
TEACHER:	So what do you think he is going to do?
CHILD:	Fly the kite.
TEACHER:	Right.

By directing the child's attention to a salient feature, namely the kite in the picture, the child was guided in his thinking to come up with the right answer. Educators call this technique scaffolding. A scaffold is a support used during the construction of a building. It's a useful analogy to describe what good teachers do when assisting children in learning situations. The teacher in the example is not only helping the child get the right answer, but is also providing support for the child to look for clues in the picture to figure out what is happening.

Level 3: Process Questions (How? Why? What Will Happen Next?)
        Why do you think he did that?
        Why do you need to wear shoes?
        Where do you think he might be going?
        What do you think will happen?
        How do you think he got in there?
        What made him so angry?

These are the most difficult, since they require the child to formulate an answer that involves explaining, predicting, and inferring. These are the types of questions parents tend to be asking more of when sharing and discussing a book with their older preschool child.

Okay, let's practice. Pick out one of your child's picture books. After looking at the book, create one or two questions for each of the levels described above.

Level 1 _____

_____

Level 2 _____

_____

Level 3 _____

_____

Chapter 8

Activity Matters

The simplest toy, one which even the youngest child can operate,
is called a grandparent.

—Sam Levinson

The best inheritance a parent can give his children
is a few minutes of his time each day.

—O. A. Battista

It has been said that play is the work of the child. It is certainly an important part of the preschooler's world. Children love when it's time to play and will readily try out most any toy or object with enthusiasm. They need time to play and the opportunity to select and become involved with a variety of activities. Unfortunately, too many preschoolers are so booked up with prearranged group activities that they are left with little free time to explore on their own. Classes in swimming, dance, crafts, gymnastics, team sports, and music can provide valuable exposure to new interests, as well as teach children how to function in a group. However, if overdone, these may reduce opportunities for free and more self-directed exploration, development of the imagination, and satisfaction of curiosity, which are so strong in the preschool years. Such highly structured situations also keep the child in the relatively passive role of listener-responder. Similarly, the latest electronic craze or toy promoted by television advertising may not be an optimum choice.

A recent article in *The New Yorker* magazine about the history of modern toys commented on the explosion of electronic gadgetry and the ways in which toys have changed, noting that many toys are geared to "entertain" and almost "play by themselves," with impressive noises and flashing lights. On the other hand, "smarter" microprocessors have also enabled the creation of educational toys and gadgets that are highly interactive. Multilingual dolls can expose young children to the sounds of foreign languages, and toys such as LeapFrog's Turbo Extreme can produce multiple-choice questions.

Although there is no reason to avoid electronic toys per se, it is helpful to consider the quality of play that will be fostered by a particular toy; there are certainly better and worse choices. Here are some questions to consider:

- How structured is the toy or game? Does it allow for lots of imagination and creativity, or is the child locked into a highly scripted format?
- What kinds of language skills does the toy or game require the child to use? For example a simple game of go fish requires taking turns, asking specific questions, listening, responding, and following a set of rules and procedures.
- What kinds of language skills can the toy or game be used to elicit? Blocks, for example, do not inherently require language, but they can be used as a basis for discussion and for imaginative play that is rich in language.
- What types of thinking does it require? Is there only one right answer, or is creative problem solving involved?
- How interactive is it? Can it be easily shared and used cooperatively by peers?

For an excellent guide to selecting age-appropriate toys and using them to promote language skills, see *The Language of Toys* and *The New Language of Toys* by Sue Schwartz.

Sometimes children who are weaker in the area of language skills take great solace in games that require only motor skills and very little talking. They tend to latch on to toys that require little or no language, such as Nintendo's Game Boys. While these toys probably do develop such skills as visual and fine-motor coordination, using them for hours on end would take away time that could be spent in other ways, for example, playing with a friend or visiting a place of interest.

Quality time at home with parents does not require the elaborate purchase of special toys. What matters is how the nature of an activity affects the development of vocabulary, grammar and other aspects of language that the child is exposed to. Different activities will place differing language demands on the child.

Blocks Versus Books: Does It Make a Difference?

The following is an exchange between a mother and her four-year-old child while playing with a set of blocks.

> MOTHER: Okay, we're gonna make this one like this. Okay? Like this.
> CHILD: Yeah.
> MOTHER: Okay. That goes like that.
> CHILD: Here [handing a block].
> MOTHER: Okay, this goes like this. Are you gonna put people on here or just animals?
> CHILD: Just animals.
> MOTHER: Okay, you could pick the animals to go inside.

Now notice how the language changes when they're sharing a wordless picture book.

> MOTHER: What is he sitting on right there?
> CHILD: A tree.
> MOTHER: A tree. Right. And what happened to the dog?
> CHILD: He fell and drowned, and his foot was up in the air. And the boy's foot was up in the air.
> MOTHER: Right. And what's that he has on his head?
> CHILD: A bucket.
> MOTHER: Why do you think he has a bucket on his head?
> CHILD: Cause he went under the water.

You probably noticed differences in the overall content and quality of the talk. In the first example, there were many nonspecific words, such as "that" and "here." The language in the second example was much richer and contained more vocabulary words. Consider the level of questions in the second example— they were much more challenging for the child and involved a lot more language.

The preceding exchanges are excerpts of transcripts I had collected for a doctoral study. Groups of mothers and their four-year-old children were videotaped in three ten-minute situations: block play, a waiting period, and looking at a picture book with no words. All the utterances were transcribed and coded as to who had initiated the topic, who had done more of the speaking, and the types of questions that were used by the parent. The results were dramatic. In the picture-book reading situation, mothers did a lot more talking, and their talk contained a significantly higher proportion of questions, in particular, process questions.

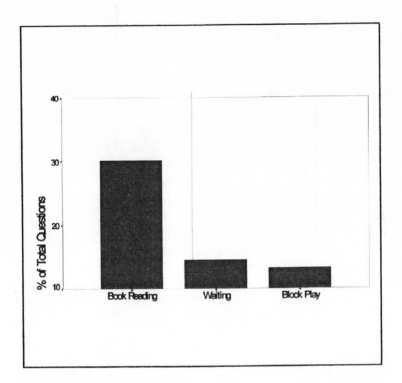

Mothers' Use of Process Questions, Expressed as a Proportion of Total Questions, Across Three Tasks

As you may have recognized, the exchange during the picture-book reading was very similar to those that occur in classrooms where the teacher is guiding a group discussion. This is another reason children who have read a lot with their parents are at a real advantage. Studies have shown a strong relationship between the amount of book reading and later language and literacy skills. Both the quantity and the quality of parents' book reading with their children matter. The types of questions parents ask their children correlate later with their children's levels of reading comprehension and abstract language development.

The point is not that blocks are bad and books are good, nor that we should only be reading with our children and nothing else. Children are learning equally important skills as they do various activities, such as block building. But when you read a book with your child, you are providing a lot of language stimulation—a kind of stimulation that differs from stimulation obtained in other types of situations. Your discussions about a book are similar to the exchanges your child will be expected to engage in at school, and will help develop the skills needed for learning to read.

Choosing and Using Books

A child's interest in books can begin in infancy. Chapters 1 through 5 contain lists of books and suggestions for using them. The strategies described in Chapter 6 are appropriate for early book-reading experiences, which can begin before the child utters his first word. Ideally, books will play a large role in the early oral-language experiences of young preschoolers. For older preschoolers, wordless picture books are a particularly good means of engaging in complex oral-language interactions as the "why" and the "what will happen" questions are discussed and shared. (For a list of wordless books, see "Using Picture Books to Promote Literacy Skills" in Chapter 10.) Read-aloud times can progress to sessions in which young nonreaders will actually "read" an entire favorite book just by mapping the oral language they have already mastered onto what they know about the nature of book reading, combined with what they know about the world and the structure of stories.

Photo: Anderson Ross / Photodisc Red / Getty Images

In *Beginning Literacy with Language,* authors David Dickinson and Patton Tabors make the following recommendations to parents:

- **Read a variety of books.** Include factual as well as fantasy books, rhyming books, and picture books. Discussions of books will vary, depending on the type of book.
- **Read books over and over again.** This helps the child become very familiar with the book and enables complex discussions.
- **Discuss the book before and after reading.** Explain unfamiliar concepts or new vocabulary before reading the book.
- **Vary intonation.** Using different voices and modifying intonation can make the book more engaging.
- **Use gestures and point to illustrations as you read.** This can help the child's comprehension without interfering with the flow of the story.
- **Have the book-reading experiences overflow into other areas.** Help the child make connections between the book and aspects of his own life by making comments and asking questions.
- **Be a reader yourself.** This provides a model for the child.

What about TV?

The American Association of Pediatrics, which comprises 55,000 doctors, published the following in its August 1999 issue of the *Journal of Pediatrics* regarding children under two years of age:

> While certain television programs may be promoted to this age group, research on early brain development shows that babies and toddlers have a critical need for direct interactions with parents and other significant caregivers for healthy brain growth and the development of appropriate social, emotional and cognitive skills.

In other words: *No* television for children under two. For children two years of age and older, the recommendation is no more than two hours a day, and parents are advised against placing televisions in children's bedrooms. My advice is this: Language development requires interaction between people. For the developing child, the ideal partner is one who can focus on the child's interests and activities. Television cannot be *responsive* to the child, and it is this responsivity that has shown itself to be a critical ingredient for language growth.

Here's a list of dos and don'ts for television:

Do

- Be selective about programs and pick ones that are well designed for children (tape for later viewing if there are time conflicts)
- Watch TV with your child and make it interactive by discussing the content
- Select a particular show that you and your child enjoy watching

Don't

- Assume that because your child is looking intently at the TV, that the program is developmentally appropriate
- Use TV as a babysitter
- Allow the child to watch for lengthy periods of time unsupervised

There are times, though, that television can be useful and educational. Consider some of these great ways to use video and/or television:

- Watch with your child. Use the remote to pause at key spots for a description, interpretation, or discussion of what has been viewed.
- Similar to book-reading suggestions, reenact a scene or activity in real life or extend the content to a related activity. Provide materials or toys that were viewed in the video or television segment. One of my favorite activities is to play a video of a *Blues Clues* segment. In my office, I set up the "thinking chair" for the child, and we draw the clues in our own "handy-dandy notebook."
- Homemade videos can provide endless ways in which to stimulate language. For example, you and your child could videotape your own "news report" or the reenactment of an imaginary play sequence.

Imaginary Play During Sensory Experiences

Materials such as paints and Play-Doh can serve as the basis for a richly stimulating language-based experience that draws upon all of the child's vocabulary and knowledge of the world. When these materials are used in an open-ended manner, children enjoy letting their imaginations run wild, and complicated story scenarios can evolve that are highly useful and stimulating.

Observe the richness of the conversation in the following interaction between children using Play-Doh:

> CHILD 1: I'm pounding mine down to make it really flat.
> CHILD 2: Yeah! Like a pancake!

CHILD 1:   Let's roll it out and make cookies!

CHILD 2:   Yeah! Chocolate chip!

CHILD 3:   Look, I'm making a fish. My fish is swimming. [Holds up the piece of Play-doh and moves it.]

Contrast this with the following dialogue—or lack thereof—overheard at a preschool when the child was completing a precut holiday project.

TEACHER: Here you go, Matthew. [Places pieces on the table next to him.] Just put the glue along here and stick this one on. [Matthew begins what he thinks is correct.]
No, no, you have it upside down. It goes *this* way. [Pulls the paper back off and replaces it.]
There you go. Now just press that down. Okay, you can put it over there on the shelf to dry.
Good job. Mommy's going to *love* that valentine.

The point here is that a project that might look adorable on your refrigerator has not necessarily been the result of the best language stimulation. (This is not to denigrate all predesigned projects, only to illustrate the potential differences in language and imagination demands that different situations can have.)

A parent complained to me, "My five-year-old son has become addicted to his Game Boy! He just wants to play with it by the hour and becomes angry when I try to take it away. What should I do?" I suggested limiting the time and discussing the reason for this with the child. I also suggested helping him find other toys or games, taking him shopping and letting him select an alternative. The use of a Game Boy can be made more interactive by having a friend over to take turns with it or having the child explain to you, as he is playing, what is happening on the screen. "Addicted" is a strong word. An addictive or obsessive behavior can sometimes be indicative of developmental issues. Consider areas that your child might not feel confident about, such as language and social skills, and find ways to promote success in these areas.

Helping Children Talk With Each Other: The Play Date

CHILD 1:   Hey, Mark, do you want to help me make a zoo?

CHILD 2:   Yeah!

CHILD 1:   Let's get those really long blocks over there for the fences. Then the animals can't get out.

CHILD 2:   And let's make a cage over here for the really dangerous animals.

CHILD 1:   Yeah.

CHILD 2: Do you want to have alligators?

CHILD 1: No. We don't have any water.

CHILD 2: But we could make a place over there for the water to be.

CHILD 1: Okay, you do the water part, and I'll do the cages.

This brief scenario is an example of how a child's social skills in the classroom will depend heavily on the child's ability to use language to do the following:

- Select partners (invite or turn down a play partner)
- Get and hold the attention of another
- Make comments
- Ask questions
- Listen and respond to the comments and questions of others
- Direct—and take direction from—others
- Discuss and formulate plans
- Make requests
- Disagree or refuse a request from another

All of these abilities will enable the child to participate successfully in play and to negotiate the course of the play scenario.

Research has demonstrated a "rich get richer and poor get poorer" phenomenon regarding the amount of social interaction among children with greater and lesser degrees of language development. Generally, the most popular and successfully interactive children tend to also be the more verbal ones. Because these children are more sought after as play partners, they tend to have more frequent opportunities for using language. Unfortunately, the reverse is also true. The less verbally capable, and often less confident, child tends to be a more peripheral group member, engaging in fewer interactions and having less of an opportunity to practice the very language skills that need to be improved.

An excellent way for a parent to help prepare the child for the complex social world of play he will encounter in the classroom is to arrange for play dates with one or two peers at a time. For a shy child, this can provide a chance to have more turns at talking, without the interruption and domination of more assertive and outgoing peers. Preschool teachers are generally very helpful in guiding parents toward good choices of playmates. Of course, the preference of your child should be a primary consideration. Don't base your choice on physical proximity. The child next door may be convenient but completely incompatible. It's well worth the effort of time and travel to select an optimum play partner. You may want to invite the child to your house first, so that you can observe the interaction. With three-year-olds, be prepared for things to get a bit bumpy, since children at this age need help learning to take turns, share, and even interact. It may help to provide them with a structured activity that will require some supervision on your part. Some ideas for these might include the following:

- Fixing and enjoying a special snack, such as pudding, cracker sandwiches, or cookies
- Creating a craft project, using clay, finger paints, beads, or colored paper
- Visiting a playground
- Playing an early-childhood board game, such as Candy Land, or a card game, such as go fish

A seasoned kindergarten teacher I know told me she advises parents to observe the three S's for having successful play dates: Keep them short, structured, and supervised.

Once your child is comfortable with a peer, he will probably be able to engage in less directed and structured activities and will cooperatively interact in fantasy or pretend play. With very few props and a suggestion or two, you will be amazed at the lively imaginative scenarios that can ensue.

Let's Pretend: Knowing the Script

Whatever the topic may be, whether it is the topic of a discussion or the theme of an imaginary play scenario, each child brings his own world knowledge to a particular task at hand. This involves knowledge of places and sequences of actions that are part of our common information base. This script, sometimes called schema, knowledge enables us to predict that, say, if the scene is a birthday party, certain items, people, and actions would be involved. There is usually a cake, the birthday song is sung, a wish is made, the candles are blown out by the birthday person, and presents are opened; there are also treats to eat and fun activities. Four-year-olds show surprising sophistication when it comes to this kind of knowledge. A four-year-old girl receiving therapy to correct an articulation problem was using a Barbie Colorforms set and practicing the word "she": "She needs a skirt," "She needs a blouse," and so forth. When I asked if Barbie needed a purse, the girl quickly responded, "Oh, no. Ken is bringing his wallet!" She had already learned a script for a date in which the guy always pays! Her mom and I shared a chuckle over her daughter's "material girl" approach.

In the preschool classroom, the play can be amusing, as scenarios are acted out and kids are imitating and revealing the social values and situations they are exposed to. One four-year-old boy, with a pretend phone to his ear, told me he was "calling to arrange lunch with a client." It is this knowledge of scripts that helps children to act out pretend-play sequences, to follow and participate in classroom discussions and, later, to derive meaning from print. It enables them to create elaborate cooperative play scenarios, complete with role playing and dialogue.

The following are examples of scripts that a child should be familiar with before entering school:

- Telephone conversation
- Farm
- Zoo
- Pet store
- Birthday party
- Library
- Construction site
- Hairdresser or barber
- Post office
- Pizza parlor
- Firehouse
- Office
- Airport
- Circus
- Vet

The script would include objects that would be present, clothing that would be worn, and specific activities and people, as well as types of dialogue, expressions, and vocabulary that might be used.

How does the child acquire script knowledge? Through participating in real-life examples, hearing about and discussing real situations, and reading about them in books or seeing them in movies or on television. In order to participate successfully, in addition to knowledge of the script, a child must be able to listen and comprehend what peers are saying, as well as to use language in order to:

- Direct—and take direction from—others
- Discuss and formulate plans
- Make polite requests
- Disagree or refuse an offer

Play dates are an excellent way for children to engage in this pretend world in a cooperative way with others. An added advantage is that an adult with one ear attuned to the interaction can help smooth out difficulties and ensure that the interaction is successful. Breakdowns may occur owing to one child not hearing or listening to the other or to a child's lack of knowing what words to use. It is at moments when words fail that children tend to resort to physical means to get their point across. Toys get grabbed away, or friends get shoved or worse! Here are some helpful adult interjections to head trouble off at the pass and avoid catastrophe (these are also useful in the preschool setting):

- **Refocusing:** "Joey said he wanted a turn. Did you hear him? Say it again, Joey."
- **Modeling:** "Joey asked if he could have a turn with the truck. You could tell him 'in just a minute.'"
- **Directing:** "I know you want to play with the truck right now, but Joey is your guest, and you need to give him a turn."
- **Allocating turns:** "I'm going to set the timer for three minutes. Then it will be Joey's turn to have the truck."
- **Rule setting:** "You just grabbed the truck away from Joey. We don't grab things from our friends. Give it back to him and use your words to ask him for it."
- **Prompting:** "You could ask Joey if he wants to go outside. Say 'Joey, do you want to go outside?'"

In case of disaster, have a back-up plan, such as suggesting another activity. When all else fails, offer a snack and a favorite video. That way, everybody gets something and no one has to talk!

Self-Check 3: Practice the Strategies

Audiotape or videotape yourself interacting with your child for a period of five to ten minutes in two contrasting situations, one of which involves discussing a picture book. (NO actual reading, please!) Play the tape back and notice the following about your language:

- Who did more of the talking—you, your child, or was it pretty balanced?
- What types of questions did you ask?
- What differences did you notice about the language in each of the situations with regard to vocabulary used, complexity of your child's sentences, and length of your child's utterances?

Consider the activities that your child is engaged in throughout the day. What types of listening and talking skills are involved? Look for the following:

- Listening and following directions
- Listening to and discussing stories

- Giving directions
- Giving explanations
- Creating stories
- Engaging in pretend play in which dialogue is created
- Conversing with peers
- Participating in group discussions

Part 3

Talking to Learn

Chapter 9

Getting Ready for School: The Preschool Experience

Children are the world's most valuable resource and its best hope for the future.
—John F. Kennedy

The only artists for whom I would make way are children. For me the paintings of children belong side by side with the works of the masters.
—Henry Miller

In some ways, classrooms are all the same, and in some ways, they are different. One of the ways in which they are the same is that the child is called upon to demonstrate his competence to the world at large.

Oh, I know! Learning to Display Knowledge in the Classroom

The following exchanges will quickly be recognized as typical of a teacher-led discussion in a classroom:

TEACHER: Sean, what day comes after Monday?
SEAN: Uh, Tuesday?
TEACHER: That's right. After Monday comes Tuesday. Very good.

TEACHER: When do we eat breakfast? . . . Charlie?
CHARLIE: In the morning.
TEACHER: That's right. We eat breakfast in the morning.

TEACHER:	Why is the girl crying? . . . Alison?
ALISON:	She's lying down.
TEACHER:	Yes, but why is she crying? What happened?
ALISON:	She got hurt.
TEACHER:	Yes, she got hurt. How did she get hurt?
ALISON:	Fall down.
TEACHER:	Yes, she fell down and got hurt, so she's crying.

In each of these examples, the teacher asks a question and selects a child to respond. Following the child's response, the teacher provides some evaluation of that response. If it is correct, it is usually affirmed in some way, often followed by further evaluation, as in the first two examples. If it is incorrect, the student is typically guided to the right response through further questions that make the answer more obvious to the student, as in the third example. Courtney Cazden, who has studied classroom talk extensively, identified this as a Q-R-E sequence—question, response, evaluation. This is a communication pattern that is very common in educational settings when the teacher is leading a group discussion.

Although this is a pattern seen in most classrooms, there are also several ways in which classrooms can differ. A classroom functions as a miniculture. Just as each human culture has variations, so does each classroom, depending on the style and personality of the teacher, the makeup of the group, and the curriculum goals of the grade or school. In one classroom, it might be necessary to raise your hand for a chance to speak, while in another, the style might be less formal, with children allowed to get the speaking floor by waiting for an appropriate pause. In some classrooms, trips to the bathroom are allowed at any time without asking, while in others, a hand must be raised and permission asked. As a child enters into membership in this special "culture," she must learn the particular behavioral expectations. These include knowing

- How to function as part of a group
- What the routines are
- When it is okay to speak, when to remain quiet
- How to get a turn at speaking
- How to get help
- How to behave and get along with peers

Learning to participate in group discussions requires a special set of skills. Unique demands are placed on attention, organization, self-control, memory, comprehension, and speaking skills. Think about what is expected of the child in this situation. First, she must be able to focus her attention on the topic at hand. She must maintain self-control as she waits for her turn to talk. She must comprehend what is being said and also remember what others have said. She must organize her own thoughts and then negotiate her turn at speaking, either by raising her hand or interjecting at an appropriate time, without interrupting someone else's turn. Finally, she must organize her words into utterances that are relevant and make sense to others in the group. These are skills that will be important throughout her school career. Some children come to the preschool classroom well equipped for the circle-time format. Children who have had experience sitting and conversing with family members at the dinner table, for example, or who have been involved in many discussions within their families are at a real advantage. Still, the discussions that take place in the home will differ from those that take place in a classroom.

The following chart lists some of the differences between the language demands of home and at school, as well as how everyday conversation differs from classroom talk.

Home/Conversation	Classroom Discussion
Less formal	More formal
Content is often about current situations or ongoing activities that provide shared knowledge for the speakers	Content often about hypothetical situations that require specific description or background information
Requires less specific vocabulary	Requires more specific vocabulary
Typically does not require analytical thinking, such as comparing, predicting, explaining	Requires analytical thinking, such as comparing, predicting, explaining
Refers frequently to present situation or context	Refers frequently to situations outside the immediate context: past, future, or hypothetical situations
No need to specify such referents as "he" or "she"	Referents such as "he," "she," or "they" need to be specified for the listener(s)
More concrete, context-bound	More abstract, context-free

But You Were the Mother Last Time: Using Language With Peers

Let's visit a corner of the room where children are playing a game together:

SEAN: I'm blue. Blue goes next.
BILLY: No. Blue goes after red.
SEAN: But red already had a turn.
BILLY: No. See, it goes red, blue, yellow, green, then red again.
SEAN: Okay, then after you go, I go.
BILLY: Yeah.

And in the housekeeping corner:

JESSICA: I'm the mother.
SAMANTHA: No, I'm the mother.
JESSICA: No, I'm the mother. Remember you were the mother last time?
SAMANTHA: Okay, then we can both be the mother.
JESSICA: No, there can't be two mothers.
RACHEL: I know! Jessica, you can be the grandmother.
JESSICA: There's no grandmother.
RACHEL: Okay, then how 'bout you and I can be sisters and Samantha
            can be the mother.
JESSICA: Okay, but next time, I get to be the mother.
SAMANTHA: Okay.

Playtime is an integral part of any preschool program. Free play involves the use of language for participation in interaction with a variety of peers and in making various choices of materials and activities. What are some of the ways a child needs to use language in this setting? In order to participate successfully, a child must, of course, be able to comprehend what other children are saying. In addition, the child must learn how to do the following:

- Attend and respond to others
- Get the attention of others or get a turn at speaking
- Exchange information
- Plan and organize actions cooperatively
- Express feelings
- Make polite requests or refusals
- Handle disagreements and resolve conflicts

Photo: SW Productions / Brand X Pictures / Getty Images

These are skills that are not only important for social development, but are also needed by adults throughout their lives. The most brilliant people don't necessarily become the most successful in life. Why? Because their people skills are poor. Conversely, studies of highly successful people have shown that they were not typically at the top of their class, nor did they have the highest IQ scores. In his autobiography, Dr. Ben Carson describes his journey from being a troubled inner-city black youth to becoming the head of pediatric neurology at The Johns Hopkins University. His premise is simple: the human brain is such an amazing organ and capable of so much that even if you only have an average one, you can be highly successful. You don't need an exceptionally high IQ. All you need is motivation and the ability to get along with people. Many of the skills you need to get along with other people begin to develop in the preschool years—and they are developed through language.

What about the child who does not come to school adept at these skills? A child with weaknesses in language can get by when he's three, because three-year-olds generally play near or next to rather than *with* others and the language demands are minimal. A three-year-old who doesn't talk at all can stand next to a peer at a sand table and share trucks, digging utensils, and sand toys and get along quite well. When three-year-olds want something, they usually just take it; turn taking and sharing can take place nonverbally. By four, however, play becomes more interactive and a language-delayed child will begin to stand out.

The following are some suggested activities to help the shy or reticent child become more verbal with peers. (For more details, see Appendix A.)

- **Table for Two.** Set up a snack corner with self-serve pitchers, cups, plates, and snacks that the children can easily serve themselves.
- **What Did You Say? (Barrier Games).** Two children sit across from each other with a barrier between them, such as a game board turned on its side. Each child is given an identical set of blocks. One child is the designated "boss" and the other the "worker." The goal is for the boss to create a design with the blocks and describe it to the worker so that the two constructions will be identical. Roles are then switched. Participants can be praised for "good listening" and "good talking."
- **Howdy, Pardner!** Here are a few partner activities:

  —Pair off children and give each pair an assignment, such as finding out information from their partner about a favorite food or toy. Then reassemble the group, and have each child report on what he found out.
  —Send the pair on an errand together.
  —Assign a collaborative project, such as creating a picture, computer graphic, or collage.
  Note: A fun way to randomize partner selection is to have several lengths of yarn or string jumbled together on the floor. The children sit in a circle and each grabs the end of one of the pieces. The person attached to the other end becomes their partner.

- **Go Fish.** Any deck of matching card pairs will do for this fun game. Create your own versions containing pairs that differ from each other only slightly so as to require more specific descriptions.

Teachers Can Help

It isn't enough just to create the situation and expect that things will develop fine on their own. The following techniques are used by well-trained teachers to help kids talk to one other:

- **Directing and Redirecting Attention.** Sometimes shy or language-delayed children tend to be ignored when they do venture forth a question or comment. An aware teacher can help by directing the attention of the child's listener by saying something like, "Sean, Matthew asked you a question. Did you hear him?" Or, "Matthew, I don't think Sean heard you. Sean, could you look at Matthew for a minute? I think he wants to ask you something."
- **Redirecting questions and comments.** Many shy children will direct requests to an adult rather than to their peer. For example, "Mrs. Dore, it's my turn to ride the bike." The adult can redirect the child by saying, "Why don't you ask Sean for a turn?"
- **Paraphrasing.** Three- and four-year-old children, and sometimes even five-year-olds, can produce very garbled messages, especially if there are glaring errors in articulation and syntax or if the meaning isn't clear. When the listener doesn't understand the child who is speaking, the teacher can help out by saying, "I think Sean is saying . . ."
- **Modeling.** If a child has trouble expressing himself because of immature language development or word-retrieval difficulties, the teacher can model the appropriate language—for example, "Say, 'Can I have a turn?'" or "Tell Michael, 'It's my turn now.'"
- **Prompting.** The teacher can prompt a child to initiate speaking by suggesting that he approach another child for some purpose—for example, "Why don't you ask Sean to play with you now?"
- **Setups.** Situations can easily be manipulated so as to require some speech on the part of the participants. For example, a snack table could be set up in such a way that plates must be passed, or an art project could be organized with only a few scissors or glue sticks, requiring that children request these objects when needed.

Sociodramatic Play

The concept of a story, comprising characters, actions, sequences of events, dialogue, and resolution of a conflict or a problem, has its roots in, and is developed through, sociodramatic play. This can include acting out simple sequences or scenarios, such as a pretend trip to the zoo or a pretend birthday party, as well as enacting a rudimentary story plot, in which there is a main character, a setting, plot development, and resolution of a problem.

A high-quality, language-based early-childhood classroom will provide many opportunities for this important activity. In *Building a Language-Focused Curriculum for the Preschool Classroom,* Mabel Rice and Kim Wilcox describe how such opportunities are built into the daily planning guide. For example, in their theme-based curriculum, if the children hear a story about an airplane trip, the art project might consist of making paper airplanes, and the song "I'm a Little Airplane" would be taught; actual items, both real and imaginary, are provided. Vocabulary covered would include such words as "pilot," "flight attendant," "baggage," "suitcase," "take-off," "landing," "seat belt," "security check," "ticket," "seat," "passenger," "beverage," and "cockpit." A theme-based curriculum creates the optimum language-based learning situation, since words and expressions are learned within contexts that involve many different sensory experiences. (See Appendix A for more specific ideas.)

Once Upon a Time: Understanding and Telling Stories

Between the ages of three and five, children are learning to use language to talk about events and experiences that are not limited by the immediate context. They are able to conceptually leave the "here and now" and conceive of "there and then." They learn to talk about past events (where they went the day before and what they did there), and future events (what they will be doing and where they will be going), as well as about abstract ideas, such as why things happen, and value judgments. As they learn to use this decontextualized, or nonimmediate, language, they are acquiring the following skills, which they will need later, when they write about experiences:

- Using grammatical elements, such as past and future tenses
- Taking the listener into account by specifying who and what they are referring to when they use such words as "it" and "he" or a person's name
- Logically sequencing ideas so that the gist of what they are saying makes sense
- Staying on a topic of conversation over the course of several turns

This shift in the ability to move away from the immediate present context and to talk about events and people displaced in time is reflected in the stories a child is able to produce. There has been a lot of research on the stories children construct Not surprisingly, there is a definite sequence of development in the structure of their stories. We can take a look at a child's story and see at what stage the child is in his story development. This can be helpful in choosing books and stories to read with the child that he will comprehend and find most appealing.

The very first stories children make up, at around age two to three, are referred to as heaps. Heaps don't have any obvious structure. They are merely a series of simple sentences describing whatever is obvious from the picture:

> The cat is lying down.
> And the boy is playing with a ball.
> And the baby is crying.

The next stage, also common in two- and three-year-olds, involves the connection of statements that are tied together by one particular character, setting, action, or feeling. Like the previous level, there are no notions of time and no causes and effects:

> Mommy in the car.
> Boy in the car.
> Daddy in a car.

The third level, called primitive narratives, involves ideas connected around a theme, but they are tied together in ways that reflect a deeper understanding of relationships and events:

> The baby is crying.
> The mommy gives her a bottle.
> The baby goes to sleep.

Later, three-, four-, and five-year-old children are able to create stories that have a series of events connected sequentially. These are called focused chains. By five, most children are able to create these. They sound more like stories because they usually have a main character who engages in a series of activities. One activity leads to another, and the only connection between the activities is that one happens after the other—there are no definite causes and effects. Although these stories are not tied to the here and now and tell about events that occurred over time, they tend to ramble on, with the ending not predictable from the beginning:

> There was a rabbit.
> And he was eating a carrot.
> And then he went for a walk.
> And then he saw a fox.
> And they went into the woods.
> And then it got dark.
> And then they went home.
> And they were tired, so they went to sleep.

True narrative structure begins to appear in children over the age of five. At this stage, their stories are recognizable as having some logical order or plot, and events are related in some causal way. Not only do they tell about "there and then" as opposed to "here and now," but in true narratives, there is usually some problem that gets resolved or some moral to the story, as in the following example:

> Once upon a time, there was a boy.
> And his name was Alex.
> And he had a pet rabbit named Fred.
> One day he went out to feed Fred, but he couldn't find him.
> Fred was gone.
> Alex looked all over for Fred.
> He finally gave up and went inside.
> He was crying.
> Then he was eating lunch, and he heard a scratching sound.
> He went to the door, and Fred was scratching on the screen.
> He hugged Fred, and everybody was so happy.
> He gave Fred lots of carrots, and he made sure Fred's cage was
>   closed up tight so he couldn't get out again.

How do children develop this sense of what a story is? By hearing them, talking about them, and creating their own. A child will be able to comprehend a much higher level of story structure than she can create. An excellent way of developing the child's concept of story structure is through the acting out of stories that have a plot and sequence—either through role playing or by using toy figures and props. This also lays the groundwork for later reading comprehension and written expression. By actually playing a role and participating in the story, the child has a much more direct understanding of what stories are all about and what constitutes a good story. Stories that lend themselves to this type of activity include *The Three Little Pigs, Little Red Riding Hood, The Three Billy Goats Gruff, Goldilocks and the Three Bears,* and *The Gingerbread Man.* (See Appendix A for more details.) Simplifying the dialogue or having the child role-play and put the idea into his own words makes the story more meaningful to the child. Alternatives to actually role-playing the parts themselves include using felt-board characters or puppet theaters, which can be set up as learning centers. A child who has a sense of how stories go will have a much easier time of understanding the stories that he will be reading and will be able to create well-written ones of his own.

The Mouse That Roars: Using Technology—
What Does the Research Say?

Computers are here to stay. In fact, lack of access to them is considered educational deprivation. According to statistics quoted in "Children and Computer Technology: Analysis and Recommendations," a special issue of *The Future of Children,* computer ownership in households with children ages two to seventeen jumped from 48 percent in 1996 to 70 percent in 2000; use of the Internet has spread nine times faster than that of radio and three times faster than that of television. Some experts have argued that computers do not belong in early-childhood classrooms and that they take precious time away from more age-appropriate activities, posing a serious detriment to children's physical, emotional, and intellectual development. But computer use is so widespread and so integral to society's functioning that the argument now is not whether but *how* computers should be used. Do computers have a place in the preschool classroom? The short answer is, as with most teaching tools, it really depends on how they are used. The following is a brief survey of what experts in educational technology have said about computers.

Computers Can Foster Social and Emotional Development

Critics have claimed that computer usage isolates children from one another. However, research has shown just the opposite. Children tend to prefer using computers with one or two partners and have been reported to spend much more time talking to peers while on the computer than when doing some other activities, such as assembling puzzles. Also, computers can foster collaborative work and can actually increase interaction between children. *Recommendation*: Place computers in the classroom next to each other and have at least two chairs in front of each monitor. Provide software that enables cooperative planning, creativity, and problem solving.

Computers Should Be Integrated Into the Curriculum

Having a separate, designated computer time as a specialty subject is like having a language time. It fragments learning in an artificial way. Computer use, like language, should be viewed as a means of learning, not as a separate designated curriculum area. The position statement issued by the National Association for the Education of Young Children (NAEYC) recommends that computers be located in the classroom rather than in a separate computer lab. It also recommends that technology be integrated into the curriculum across subject-matter areas; for example, a computer can be used to make signs for a pretend restaurant in dramatic play. Experts suggest that preschool children be given many opportunities to explore open-ended, developmentally appropriate software within a play context.

Computers can offer a rich medium when integrated into specific curriculum areas:

- **Reading and Writing.**
  When children are collaborating, they are using language—some research has shown that a child uses twice as many words per minute at the computer with a peer than during other activities. Computers lend themselves to partner activities. With computer-based interactive storybooks, a wide range of emergent literacy skills are affected, including sound and print awareness, predicting and sequencing, letter recognition, and understanding of concepts. Many programs offer a means of connecting talk with text that can empower emergent readers and writers. Digital cameras can be used to create multimedia documentation of class projects and trips. Computers can provide the opportunity for children to author their own books. Children's story dictations can be typed in large-print sentences at the bottom of pages, then printed out for illustration by the child.

  For children who need extra support, there are direct tutorial types of programs designed to promote the development of spoken language. Laureate makes software designed specifically for the development of vocabulary, concepts, categorization, sentence structures, and narrative production. Cognitive Concepts produces a software program called *Earobics,* which targets auditory skills associated with phonemic awareness and reading readiness. (See Appendix B for additional resources.)

- **Mathematics**
  Use of computer manipulatives in conjunction with physical manipulatives can contribute to early mathematics education.

- **Art**
  Kid Pix (see Appendix B) and other programs have been recommended as an excellent way to provide open-ended exploration using a computer, and some programs have the capability to provide options for sound and voice recording as well.

- **Research or Field Trips**
  Age-appropriate Web sites and information-based software programs, such as *Encarta Encyclopedia,* can empower children to use the computer as a research tool before they learn to do this more formally in the higher grades. Other programs, such as *Nature-Virtual Serengeti* (Disney Interactive), or online network connections with children in

other classrooms, cities, and even countries enable virtual field trips using the Internet.

Limit Time Spent Looking at a Monitor

The American Academy of Pediatrics (AAP) recommends that the total time in front of screens, including television, video-games, and computer-monitors, should be limited to no more than two hours a day. Children need physical activity and interaction with peers in other social situations, such as pretend play. Excessive time in front of a television screen is not healthy for growing children and has been linked to obesity.

Choose Software Carefully

Using computers for the sake of using them is inappropriate, and an educational plan should be in place before expensive hardware systems are installed. Software that enriches, and can be integrated into, the content of the curriculum is preferable. The International Society for Technology in Education *(www.iste.org)* publishes reviews that rate programs for quality. Open-ended programs tend to promote cooperation and collaboration, while drill-and-practice programs tend to be more competitive in spirit. Mindless drills or violent video games can be detrimental.

Monitor Home Computer Use

A survey found that half of all children using the Internet at home lack any parental restrictions on the total time they spend online and the sites they visit. Parents need to be informed about monitoring tools to help keep children safe from harmful content or sexual predators and must take an active role in supervising their child's computer usage. (For a recently published resource, see Simon Johnson's *Keep Your Kids Safe on the Internet.*)

In summary, while computers will hopefully never replace tried-and-true early-childhood materials, such as blocks, paint, and water tables, they are immensely powerful educational tools which young children find intrinsically compelling. It is up to parents and educators to choose high-quality, developmentally appropriate software for the children in their care.

What to Look For in a Preschool

Rather than searching for the ideal curriculum, experts in early-childhood education say that you should look at basics first. Laura Justice, an associate professor of early-childhood education at the University of Virginia, recommends looking at what she calls a "first tier of excellence" before considering specific instructional support. What is the overall "feel" of the setting? Is there a warm positive atmosphere? Do the teachers seem to enjoy what they're doing? Do the children's contributions appear to be valued? The following are other attributes that parents should look for:

- Teachers nurture language and communication skills by encouraging conversation; they talk with the children a lot and provide opportunities for children to talk with one another.
- Teachers set clear limits about acceptable behavior but are not bossy or overcontrolling.
- There is a planned routine or schedule, but children are not rushed or forced to sit for long periods of time.
- The classroom is arranged so that children have access to toys with appropriate materials and are given opportunities for pretend play.
- Adults read to the children every day and help children talk about what is read, relating it to other aspects of their lives.
- Parents are welcomed into the classroom and are valued as an important part of the child's education.
- Age-appropriate preliteracy skills are being taught in a systematic and purposeful way.

Chapter 10

Getting Ready to Read and Write:

It's Not as Simple as ABC

The person who moves a mountain begins by carrying away small stones.
—Chinese Proverb

"Begin at the beginning," the king said, gravely,
"and go 'til you come to the end; then stop."
—Lewis Carroll

The roots of becoming a successful reader lie in the solid foundation of good oral-language development. In other words, in general, the better you are at oral language skills, the easier it will be to learn to read. (The exception to this rule is children who have visual problems; though such children make up a relatively small minority of poor readers, they do exist.) Simply teaching the names of the letters and the sounds they make, while important, is not going to make the child a good reader.

The Language-Literacy Connection

When a child encounters a word printed on a page, all of the child's knowledge of the real world, as well as his knowledge of language, will be brought to bear to "decode" any given word. Let's say you are trying to read a book about a zoo. If you have some experience with a zoo and some knowledge of letter sounds, you would be better able to decipher the following:

The zookeeper fed the l_____ns, b____rs, z_____s, el_____ts, m_____s, and the s_____ls.

Try filling in the missing words in this sentence:

The seals were sw_____ing in the w___r and b___l___g balls on their
n___s. The m_____es were e_____ing ba_____s.

Your knowledge of the world and your language skills helped you figure out the words that you weren't sure of. If you know that seals swim in water and that monkeys eat bananas, you are at an advantage. It is this same process that the beginning reader is applying. The more vocabulary a child knows and the more he knows about how the world works and how sentences go, the easier it will be to read the words when he sees them on the page, because he will have an idea of what the next word will probably be. Of course, a successful reader will also be able to associate the letters with sounds, or phonemes, and be able to blend them together. You may not have been aware when reading the examples that you also needed to jump back and forth between thinking about the meaning of the sentence and stopping to figure out the missing letters or sounds. This ability to hold on to and think about these two different aspects of language at the same time is one reason younger children may not yet be ready to read, even when they know all of the sounds of the letters.

It has been well established in the research literature that weak language skills put a child at risk for learning problems. Functioning in a classroom involves being able to listen and comprehend language spoken by the teacher and peers and requires the use of language to express ideas and give responses to questions. It has also been well established that problems in language development often give rise to problems with reading and writing. Conversely, strengths in oral language are highly correlated with later success in leaning to read. To understand why this is so, it is helpful to look at how the child learns to read.

Books Tell Stories

Before a child even looks at printed words, she needs to get the idea that books tell stories or provide information. How does she do that? Through all of the interactive book reading that has been going on with her parents. Usually, before a child learns to actually read words, it is common to see the child sitting with a book, pretending to read. This is called print awareness. Children know that the writing represents the words that tell the story. They sound like they are reading, but they are just making up words to go along with the pictures. This can be encouraged by providing them with lots of simple picture books or books with no words at all, only pictures.

Wordless books are an excellent way to bridge the world of "telling" stories with the world of actually reading.

Using Picture Books to Promote Literacy Skills

Wordless picture books are great for interactive story reading. The meaning must be gleaned from the pictures, enabling the reader to think out loud and create the text orally through discussion with the adult. These books are great for getting children to talk! They pave the way for good comprehension, because they stress that the reader has to do some of the work to figure out how the story goes. Here are a few titles of books that have only pictures:

- *The Snowman* by Raymond Briggs
- *Peter Spier's Rain* by Peter Spier
- *Picnic* by Emily Arnold McCully
- *School* by Emily Arnold McCully
- *A Boy, a Dog and a Frog* (one in a series of several frog books) by Mercer Mayer
- *Good Dog, Carl* (one in a series of Carl books) by Alexandra Day
- *Pancakes for Breakfast* by Tomie DePaola

Photo: Comstock Images / Getty Images

Make-It-Yourself Books and Books on Tape

Homemade books are an excellent way to combine oral-language skills with exposure to printed material. Here are a few suggestions:

- Photograph a daily sequence (for example, getting ready for school or bed) or a special trip or vacation. Take some blank sheets of paper and glue one picture on each sheet. Narrate the story with your child, writing down the words you say under each picture. Tape-record the book; prompt your child to record each sentence one at a time. Your child will love hearing himself read a story—especially one about him!
- Tape-record yourself reading a favorite book with your child. At the appropriate places, record the words "Okay, now we turn the page," or have your child make a special sound at each turn of the page. (He can bang on something, blow a whistle, or make a certain sound.) Place the tape and book in a clear plastic food-storage bag, preferably one with a zipper, and hang the bag on a hook near his tape player. Several of these can be stored on hooks, creating a listening center. You can also tape-record your discussion about the book for later listening.
- Use commercially available sequence cards or pictures that can be photocopied (see *Fold a Book*, listed in Appendix B), cut out, and glued on separate cards. These can be mixed up, then placed on the floor or table in left-to-right order, with the child telling the story as he proceeds from one card to the next. (They can be placed in a small bag or box for storage, with a rubber band around each set of story cards for easy use.)
- After a special trip or experience that the child will enjoy talking about, sit down at the computer with your child. Make the font size *very* large (at least 24 points). Scroll down to the bottom of the page and have the child dictate one simple sentence about the experience. Go to the next page, scroll down, and type the next sentence your child dictates. Once you have about five to eight blank pages, each with a large sentence at the bottom, print them out. Then sit with your child and read each page; let your child create his own drawing to illustrate the sentence. Create a title page on a blank piece of paper and then staple the pages to form a book. *Voilà!*

Three Easy Homemade Books:

- Use a blank 8½- x 11-inch paper. Fold in half and then in half again. Staple the folded side and cut along the other folded edge so that the pages can turn freely. You now have a small book with eight blank pages.
- For a larger book, staple together entire blank pages. For extra durability, you can place the pages in clear page protectors with ready-made holes

for a binder. Use a round metal ring to bind the pages together once they have been created and placed in the protectors.

- Cut a 3-inch-wide strip of 8- x 14-inch paper and fold accordion-style. (See the description of stick-writing stories in the "Early Writing Development" section later in this chapter.)

Using Words to Talk About Words and Sounds: Metalinguistics

Children learn to talk without any conscious effort or awareness. This is not true of learning to read. To become literate, children must learn that the seamless flow of spoken language can be broken down into smaller segments and that the things we call "words," "sentences," and "sounds" can be represented by written letters. This is called metalinguistic awareness ("meta" meaning "above" or "outside")—viewing language itself as an object to be segmented, thought about, and talked about. A child who knows that "Catherine" is a longer name (or has more letters) than "Mike" is demonstrating this awareness, as is the child who says, "'Cake' has the same sound as my name, 'Catherine,'" or the one who says, "Hat, bat—they rhyme!" The keys to unlocking the "code" of written language include the following insights:

- **Words are things that have certain features.** Words can be spoken or written and are entities that have meanings. Words can be grouped into categories, such as animals. Words can be opposites, such as "little" and "big." A word can mean more than one thing; for example, "can" may refer to the verb meaning "to be able," or to the container. There is a high correlation between a child's ability to define a word and later reading success. An excellent activity to promote this ability is to play a guessing game. Picture cards of items from various categories can be laid out on a table and, if desired, sorted into rows by category. Players take turns giving a clue that contains the category name (for example, "It's an animal") and one or two features of the item (for example, "It lives in a jungle and has stripes"). Further examples of activities designed to build awareness in this area can be found in Appendix A under "Semantic Skills."
- **Words are separate from their meanings.** We take this knowledge for granted, but to a very young child, a "long" word may be one that refers to something physically long, like "river." One of the items on an articulation test is the word "telephone." When a child I was testing called it a "phone," I said, "Could you say it the longer way?" at which point he stretched out the word, saying, "Phooooooone."
- **Words can be put together to make sentences, and correct sentences have a certain order.** For example, we don't say "the blue, big ball" or "Where he's going?" The sentence "The boy kicked the _____" will most likely

involve a kickable object in the blank space. Predictable storybooks are useful for drawing attention to this aspect of language—for example, books with repetitive sentence structures, such as "Brown Bear, brown bear, what do you see? I see a _____ looking at me." An excellent resource for creating your own predictable books is *Storymaking*, available from Thinking Publications. The book contains reproducible materials for modifying well-known predictable books from children's literature.

- **Sentences, like words, can be long or short.** A good activity for developing awareness of sentence structures is to have children start with a short kernel sentence created by looking at a picture, then take turns adding more and more words. This enables practice of many sentences forms. For example, one child might draw a picture card and start off with "He walked." At the prompting of the teacher, who says, "Where?" the next child might add, "He walked to the store." The teacher might call for "When." The next child might say, "He walked to the store on Friday." The next question might be "Why?" A correct response might be "He walked to the store on Friday to get some milk."

- **Sentences can be broken down into words.** Sentence segmentation activities can help a child hear the individual words in a sentence. Use blocks, coins, poker chips, dominoes, or Unifix cubes. The child listens to a sentence of three to seven words and places a token on the table (left to right) in front of him for each word. He repeats the sentence, touching a token as he says each word.

- **Words can be broken apart into smaller parts called syllables.** Clapping or tapping out syllables of a word helps the child hear the syllable segments of words. Words can have ending parts or beginning parts that change their meaning (stopped/stopping, school/preschool, tie/untie).

- **Syllables can be broken apart into individual sounds, or phonemes.** The child's developing awareness of the way words sound is a major milestone and the key that opens the secret inner chamber of the magical world of books and print. It is the mapping of these sounds onto the actual ABC's that enables a child to see a word for the first time, even a nonsense word, and decode it by blending the sounds the letters make into a word. It is precisely the lack of this skill that has now been discovered to be the major culprit in the reading disorder dyslexia. Conversely, children who show solid early ability in the area of phonemic awareness generally go on to become good readers.

To become a successful reader, all of the preceding skills need to become integrated so that the child can simultaneously think from top down (knowledge of the world and general information) and bottom up (knowing the individual sounds that letters make and being able to blend them together to form a meaningful word).

Phonemic Awareness

Many children learn to "crack" the alphabet code on their own. As they pay attention to the letters in written words and match or compare their knowledge of how a word sounds with their knowledge of the letters of the alphabet, they can figure out that when they see the letter *s,* for example, it is going to signal that the word starts with *sssss.* They begin to manipulate parts of words and can talk about the "beginning sound" or the "sound at the end of the word." This awareness of the sounds that words are made up of is phonemic awareness. Many children develop and use this awareness without much direct teaching. The whole-language approach to reading was based on this assumption. The thinking went like this: If the child has a lot of world knowledge, a good command of oral language, and a love of books, the process of learning to read will automatically take place, and we needn't bother with boring skills-based work, such as traditional phonics. However, we now know that this assumption has shortchanged the approximately one third of children who, for whatever reason, will need more explicit instruction in the sound system of English because of their lack of phonemic awareness.

A common item on phonemic awareness tests, which are used to measure how aware a child is of word parts, is a syllable-deletion task. The tester says, "Say airplane." The child repeats the word. The examiner then says, "Now say it again, but don't say 'plane.'" The child is supposed to say "air." Children who are not tuning in to this aspect of words and their parts have a hard time with these types of items. One boy I was testing was having trouble with this item. When asked to "Say it again, but don't say 'plane,'" he was stumped. When I prodded, "What do you get when you take away 'plane'?" He looked at me quizzically and responded, "Sky?" I realized he was thinking about removing "plane" not from the *word,* but from his image of a plane in the sky. Difficulty with these types of tasks can be an early warning sign of later reading difficulties. Other signs include difficulty retrieving words when speaking and errors in sequencing sounds in words. Most children make some sound-order errors (as in "buhsketti" for "spaghetti" or "aminal" for "animal"), but when these are frequent and occur in simpler words, it may be a warning sign. The errors can make for cute stories, however. When I was teaching, one little boy in my special-education first-grade class was particularly proud of being able to recite the Pledge of Allegiance. My teacher's aide and I had a chuckle when we heard him blurt out, "And to the republic for Richard Stands!" Another day, the entire school was gathered out on the front lawn for a dedication ceremony of the new thoroughfare for buses. It was to be called Constitution Way. There was a long delay in getting the ceremony started, and when one of my students asked, "Why are we waiting?" another piped up, without any idea of how funny she was being, "For Constipation Way!"

What are the components of phonemic awareness, and how can one foster its development?

Phonemes are the smallest units that a spoken word can be segmented into. Placing all or too much emphasis on this level too soon (for example, drilling letter-sound memorization) is to ignore the child's need to develop awareness of the larger chunks of language, which usually develops first. One precursor to phonemic awareness is awareness that a spoken sentence is made up of units called words and that the speech stream can be segmented into these units. Using blocks or pennies or other small objects, the child can be shown how to represent each of the spoken words of a sentence with an object or a squiggle written on a page to describe a picture. Tapping or clapping out the words can also be done.

Another precursor is awareness that words have parts, or syllables. This can be demonstrated to children by having them clap or beat out the syllables of their own names, the names of characters, or the names of animals. It's best to start with compound words; these are easier to break apart, since each syllable is a recognizable word. Here are some examples:

bobcat	raindrop	mailman
snowball	raincoat	driveway
snowflake	meatball	doormat
snowboard	cupcake	cowboy
snowman	firehouse	fruitcake
fireman	boyfriend	baseball
football	airplane	airport
grapefruit		

You can make up riddles to turn this into a fun activity—for example, "I'm not a cow, and I'm not a boy, but put them together, and you'll know my name."

The next level of difficulty is to have the child segment one- to five-syllable words into their parts. A fun activity to teach this skill is to take animal picture cards and a jar of pennies. A player draws a card and places a penny on a table for each part heard. For example, "bird" would only have one penny, whereas "orangutan" would have four. Each player places the pennies in his or her bank; the player with the most wins. Here is a list of one- to five-syllable animal words:

e-le-phant (3)	ze-bra (2)	kan-ga-roo (3)
cro-co-dile (3)	ca-mel (2)	oc-to-pus (3)
a-lli-ga-tor (4)	li-on (2)	cow (1)
rhi-no-ce-ros (4)	mon-key (2)	horse (1)
hip-po-po-ta-mus (5)	gi-raffe (2)	pig (1)

Rhyming

One of the earliest manifestations of the child's growing awareness of the sound patterns of words is in the ability to appreciate and enjoy rhyming word patterns. Exposure to, and appreciation of, rhyming can begin as early as two years of age. Old favorite nursery rhymes or Dr. Seuss books are fun ways to help your child develop a sense of the sound patterns of rhyming. A child must first have exposure to, and be able to hear a lot of, rhyming words in order to be able to recognize them or to create them. Once the child is familiar with the lines of a poem or story, have him fill in the blank with the rhyming word as you start the sentence— for example, "Jack and Jill went up the . . ." Here are some other ways to help your child get the idea of rhyming:

- Collect an example of each of the following objects and place them in a box: goat-boat, rock-sock, bug-mug, lock-block, car-jar, bear-chair, log-frog, parrot-carrot, hat-cat, bell-shell, dish-fish, house-mouse, man-pan, boy-toy, hook-book, tree-bee. Take a few out at a time and help the child find the rhyming pairs: Then have the child find the rhyming pairs on his own. A great game for the car is to pick a word, then take turns rhyming it until no one can think of any more. Or pick a word and go through the alphabet, changing each of the first sounds of the word by using the next letter—for example, at, bat, cat, dat, fat, gat, and so on.
- Use rhyming picture cards, which are commercially available from educational companies. Place three cards on the table and help the child figure out which two rhyme. Put the rhyming pairs together. Once all have been sorted, repeat the rhyming word pairs: Say one word, and have the child respond with the other. Give the child lots of examples, so he has a chance to hear what rhyming is. If the child still has trouble, say, "Watch my finger." Move your finger to your mouth as you say each word, exaggerating the word ending when your finger reaches your mouth. Another version of this is to play a fishing game.

Place a paper clip on each card, then place the cards faceup on the table or floor. Create a fishing pole with a chopstick, string, and magnet. Have the child fish for rhyming pairs. A more challenging game with rhyming cards is to play go fish. Take turns asking if the other player has a word that rhymes with a word you have selected. Or place the cards facedown, and play a memory game, taking turns turning over two cards at a time. If they match (that is, rhyme), the player gets to take them and gets another turn.

Phonemic Segmentation

This is a critical skill for the development of early reading and spelling. The child develops the ability to say a word and segment it into its individual sounds. This skill usually begins around kindergarten age and progresses through the early grades. It is both a requirement for, and a by-product of, formal reading instruction. An example of this skill is to have the child say the word "cat," and then say each letter sound separately—for example, *c-a-t*. (Each sound can be represented by a poker chip or a block.)

An easier task, more appropriate for preschool, is to have the child identify words that begin or end with the same sound. For example, say to the child, "Listen to these words. They all begin with *sssss,* but one doesn't belong: 'soap,' 'sandwich,' 'mop,' 'sun.'" Or "Which word begins with the *sssss* sound: 'cap' or 'sun'?" A slightly higher-level task would be to ask the child to isolate the beginning sound of a word. For example, ask the child, "What's the beginning sound of 'sun'?" There are many commercially available materials to help develop the child's awareness of sounds in words.

Phonemic Synthesis

Phonemic synthesis, or sound blending, is a skill that involves hearing the individual phonemes of a word and blending them together. For example, the child would be presented with "*P-o-p* . . . What word did I say?" It is the opposite of segmenting the word. This skill is usually developed by the end of kindergarten.

Phoneme Deletion

Phoneme deletion requires the child to leave out an individual sound in a word. For example, tell the child, "Say 'pan.' Now say it again, but don't say *p*." This task is much more difficult and would not be expected until late kindergarten or early first grade. Much of this skill develops in tandem with the direct teaching of letter sounds that is part of the reading-readiness curriculum of most kindergartens. The precursor to this task would be syllable deletion, in which the child is asked, for example, to say a word such as "umbrella" and then to say it again, without the "um."

Substitution of Phonemes

This task is highly predictive of a child's readiness to read. Colored blocks are used to represent individual sounds, and the child is asked to change one word into another by replacing the appropriate block. For example, instruct the child, "If this is 'pat,' show me 'rat' [or 'pan' or 'pot']." To change "pat" to "rat," the child must remove the first of the three blocks and replace it with another block of a different color. To change "rat" to "ran," the last block would be replaced with a different-color block. Once a child can conceptualize, represent, and manipulate the individual sounds in words, he should have no trouble learning to read. It's a simple step to substitute a printed letter instead of a colored block, since the underlying principle is the same.

Phoneme-Grapheme Correspondence

At some point, usually in kindergarten or first grade, children develop what is called phoneme-grapheme, or sound-symbol correspondence, in which they not only can name a letter of the alphabet, but can also identify the sound it makes. Playing with letter tiles to invent words is an enjoyable activity at this stage. Once children have learned to form words by themselves, they usually like to "write" real words by creating lists, pretend letters, notes, recipes, and restaurant orders.

The names of the letters are generally learned first. For some fun activities to help the child learn the names of the alphabet letters, see the "Top Ten Activities for Ages Five to Six" at the end of Chapter 5. To help the child learn the sound each letter makes, here is an activity you can try: Gather a few coffee cans or boxes. Tape a large capital alphabet letter on the outside of the can or box, and place objects inside it that begin with that sound. For example, in the *B* container, you might have a ball, button, bottle, and a toy bear. Dump the objects out and sort them back into the containers according to their beginning sounds. For example, "bear" starts with *b,* so that goes in the *B* can.

The same kind of sorting activity can be done with picture cards and letter tiles. Gather a few pictures, Place a letter tile on the table and help the child find the pictures that start with the sound that the letter makes. A good car game is to pick a letter sound and take turns thinking of words that begin with that sound until you run out. (See Appendix A for more activities.)

Matching Words to Print

The long road to literacy usually begins with the child's recognition by sight of common signs and symbols (fast-food logos, stop signs, toothpaste containers, soda-can labels) and of simple or familiar words such as his name. As the child encounters more and more words, the sound segments of the words become associated with, or mapped onto, the letters in the printed word he sees. Knowledge of these sound-symbol correspondences (or letter sounds) is *one* of the tools the child will use to decode, or figure out, what a word says. As was previously mentioned, other aspects of language come into play in decoding, such as knowledge of vocabulary, word parts, and sentence patterns. Once a word has been decoded a number of times, it becomes automatically recognizable, and the sounding out need no longer occur. Approximately one third of children in the early grades will need direct instruction in letter sounds and assistance in learning the decoding process. Commercially available programs, such as Lindamood and PAF (Preventing Academic Failure), are helpful for such children. The child is taught the letter sounds and is then presented with highly controlled patterned words, such as "bat," "rat," "fat," and "sat," in order to make the decoding process more obvious.

Reading Comprehension

It is possible for a child to learn to become a skilled decoder, calling out the words on the page and not understanding what she has read. This is an issue of reading comprehension. While dyslexia typically involves a problem with matching the underlying sound patterns of words with their printed counterparts, there are a number of poor readers who have trouble only with comprehension. Researchers are finding that many poor comprehenders have underlying weaknesses in areas of language that have gone undetected because they are subtle. In fact, it is reported that the vast majority of poor comprehenders have related low language ability.

Early Math Concepts

Just as learning to read is more complicated than learning the ABC's, a child's readiness in math is more than merely learning to recite numbers. In addition to learning the number names, the child must develop one-to-one correspondence—saying one number for each item that is counted. Success with math also requires an understanding of many concepts, such as those involving quantity, comparisons, spatial relations, time, and seriation, that is, placing items in a series of increasing size, length, and so forth. Since these concepts have words that refer to them, they involve language and the understanding of certain vocabulary. The following are concepts appropriate for children prior to kindergarten entry.

Earlier-developing concepts

These concepts are usually comprehended fairly easily by children age three to four:

Top	First	Down	On	Next to	Up
Highest	Under	Nearest	In front of	Many	One
More	Most	Same	Different	In back of	Another

Later-developing concepts

These concepts are usually comprehended fairly easily by children ages four to five:

Last	Before	After	Next	Bottom	Toward
Middle	Across	Between	Second	Third	Finished
Over	Least	A few	Through	Around	

Photo: Photodisc Collection / Photodisc Blue / Getty Images

Jean Piaget, the well-known child psychologist, studied how children's thinking shifts at about six years of age. At around this age, he found them capable of concrete operations, hence the term "concrete operational stage" of thinking. The child comes to realize that the actual number or quantity of items can remain the same, no matter how the items are placed or spaced apart. To see whether or not a child has reached this stage, you can try the following experiment: Place six pennies in a row on the table, and have the child count them. Then count out six more pennies, but space them farther apart. Ask the child which line has more pennies. A younger child will be fooled, thinking that the line that looks longer has more pennies. But if the child can tell you that both lines have the same number, he has successfully completed what is called a conservation-of-number task. For other tasks to determine a child's stage of thinking development, consult *Piagetian Activities: A Diagnostic and Developmental Approach* available from Thinking Publications.

Another important skill in math is to be able to comprehend and do math problems that are presented as short storylike segments that typically incorporate many of the concepts mentioned earlier. Math story problems involving the numbers zero to five can be acted out with real objects and toys during everyday activities, such as eating: "Michelle had three cookies. Then she ate one. How many were left?" Or, "If you have three M&M's and I give you two more, how many will you have?" Or, while playing with stuffed animals: "There were four animals sitting on the bed. Two fell off. How many were left?" Or, "Once there were two animals sitting on the pillow. Then two more came. How many are there on the bed now?"

Early Writing Development

At about age five, children begin to express an interest in forming letters and in writing. Usually this begins with the desire to learn to write their name. Developmentally, the child acquires motor patterns from gross toward fine in a process of refinement. In other words, large motor movements, such as moving the entire arm in space, are easier than the smaller refined movements of fingers manipulating a pencil. Therefore, readiness activities for writing should capitalize on this by using materials that allow for larger-scale production of letters.

Prewriting Activities

The child should be encouraged to explore motor patterns through such activities as the following:

- Drawing with a stick on wet, packed sand
- Finger painting with pudding, Jell-O powder, or whipped cream on a cookie sheet
- Finger painting with shaving cream on bathroom tiles
- Drawing with wet brushes on a blackboard
- Drawing on wipe-off boards with dry-erase markers
- Pouring sand or colored sugar from a narrow funnel onto a tray
- Drawing on a sidewalk with large chalk
- Squeezing tubes of cake-decorating gel onto waxed paper

Patterns and Shapes

The following are some general age-level expectations for copying shapes:

- Cross   two years
- Circle   three years
- Square   four years
- Triangle   five years
- Diamond   six years

Beginning to Form Letters

It is generally better to start with uppercase letters first and then proceed to lowercase. It's best if the child learns to form the letters from the top down, since this makes the handwriting process easier, though many young children will insist on going the other way. Straight up-and-down lines are easier than slanted lines to start with: **L T I P B D**. Try to have the child learn the counterclockwise motion for forming such letters as **c o d g q**. This will make letter formation easier in the long run. If you start with a *C*, it will make sense to start the same way for the O; each of the remaining letters can be formed by starting in the same way, which enables each to be written without lifting the pencil.

An obvious place to start is to use the child's name. There are many fun ways to help the child learn to recognize the patterns that make up the letters of his name. Using glitter, pretzel pieces, broken pieces of raw pasta, or other materials, create letter formations that can be glued to a piece of wood, cardboard, or other flat surface. Make a sign for the door of the child's room or a plaque for the wall. Another fun activity is to decorate cookies with cake-decorating gel. These come in bright colors, and the tubes are easy for the child to grasp and squeeze.

General Guidelines for Encouraging Writing Development

- Create a print-rich environment with labels.
- Engage the child in your own printing activities, such as writing grocery lists, "to do" lists, and notes. A few more ideas for meaningful writing:
  —List of rules
  —Weekly menu
  —Birthday-party guest list
  —Holiday present list
  —Address book of friends with phone numbers
  —Places to visit
  —Message in a bottle

> —Treasure-hunt clues
> —Love notes
> —Secret messages

- Set up a writing center area for your child, in which the following are easily accessible:

> —Small chalkboard with colored chalk
> —Wipe-off board with markers
> —Magnetic letters
> —Cards, paper, and small blank books
> —Markers, pencils, crayons, and pens
> —Postage stamps, stickers, and envelopes
> —Ink pad and stamper, tape, glue, scissors

- Avoid coercing the child into learning to write, and stay away from workbooks.

Scribble Writing

A child's first attempts at writing words on paper may just be little squiggles as he says the words out loud. This should be encouraged, since it will improve the control of holding and maneuvering a pencil and give the child the feeling of empowerment that writing can bring. Adults can model scribble writing by making a series of wavy lines in a left-to-right progression, with spaces left in between. This will reinforce the idea of segmenting spoken sentences into words.

Invented Spelling

The next phase of early writing development is the use of actual alphabet letters to represent the sounds in the words the child is trying to write. Just knowing the names of some letters can enable a child to write many words, since the names of most letters contain the same sound they represent. (For example, the name of the letter *B* starts with the sound *b*.) Children can be encouraged to put down the sounds they hear in the words they are trying to write. Don't worry that the word is spelled incorrectly. It's more important at this early stage to support the attempts and not try to correct what is produced. There will be plenty of time for that later. Just enjoy your child's first attempts at recording his own words. Expect many amusing creations, such as "MiBKZNU," one four-year-old's attempt at writing "My bike is new."

Stick-Writing Stories

One technique that has been used successfully with language- and learning-impaired children is to have them draw simple pictures to depict the sentences they are trying to write. I like to take a strip of paper about two inches wide and fourteen inches long (or you can glue together two strips of eleven-inch paper) and fold it accordion-style to make a booklet. I start a story, ("Once there was a little girl . . .") and have the child make a drawing of a little person on the first page. Each page is illustrated with very primitive stick drawings to depict the events in the story. It is surprising how easy it is for the child to then "read" the story out loud after it is completed.

Making Books for the Classroom

Creating books about students and events in the classroom is an engaging activity for preschool—and kindergarten-age children. Digital cameras and software programs make it easy to create books on a variety of topics, such as

- Our Trip to _____ [the Zoo, the Museum, the Beach]
- Our Cooking Project
- _____'s Birthday
- Our Class Pet
- Halloween in Our Class
- All About [child's name]

Some classrooms have a student of the week. It is fun to create a book about this student by having each member of the class illustrate and write down (or dictate to an adult) words that tell about this classmate.

Favorite storybooks can be modified and a classroom version created, substituting the names of children in the class for some of the characters. *Popcorn* by Frank Asch is a book that lends itself to such a project, since the story mentions by name several friends who get together for a Halloween party. When someone accidentally pours the whole bag of popcorn in the pot, the situation gets out of control! Such books can be read out loud, with each child reading a particular page. A tape recording of this can be placed in a zippered plastic bag and stored in the reading and listening corner for independent replay by students.

Another fun idea is to make up a group story by having several children sit around a tape recorder and create a story one sentence at a time. Such stories can be open-ended, or you can give structure by letting each child fill in the blank in sentences you have provided, such as, "Once there was a _____. His name was _____. He was very _____. He liked to _____. One day he was _____ing when _____." Have the students create some problem situation, and provide the sentences to solve the problem. Have everyone shout "THE END!" together at the end of the story. Children love hearing their own voices. If it is a particularly good story, let each child illustrate a page, and store the book and tape for later listening.

Developmental Milestones for Literacy Acquisition

The following are some benchmarks to help you know what to expect in a child's language development at different ages. This information was obtained primarily from research by Catherine Snow and her colleagues, as well as from the work of Sally Shaywitz. The information is general and not written in stone. A lack of any one particular behavior is not necessarily indicative of a problem.

Birth to Age Three
- Recognizes specific books by their covers
- Understands that books are objects that are handled differently from other objects
- Participates in book-sharing routines with the caregiver
- Labels objects in books
- Listens to stories

Early Preschool Accomplishments (Ages Three to Four)
- Shows an interest in books and reading
- When being read a story, connects content to life experiences
- Begins to develop awareness of the sounds of language
- Begins to develop awareness that sentences and words can be broken down into smaller parts
- Can play with the sounds of words, enjoys rhymes, can recite nursery rhymes ("Humpty Dumpty," "Jack and Jill")
- Knows that alphabet letters have unique visual patterns
- Identifies ten alphabet letters, most likely from his or her own name
- Knows that the printed part of the page is what is being read
- Pretends to write or scribbles messages during play

Late Preschool Accomplishments (Ages Four to Five)
- Can break a spoken word into its component syllables (for example., "cup-cake"); 50 percent of children can count the number of syllables in a spoken word
- Begins to be able to break up words into phonemes; 20 percent of children can count the number of phonemes in a spoken word
- Recognizes and names a growing number of letters

Beginning Kindergarten Accomplishments (Ages Five to Five and a Half)
- Compares whether two spoken words rhyme: Do "cat" and "mat" rhyme? Do "hop" and "mat" rhyme?
- Names a word that rhymes with a simple word, like "cat" or "make"
- Recognizes and names just about all upper- and lowercase letters

End of Kindergarten Accomplishments (Ages Five and a Half to Six): Spoken language
- Retells, reenacts, or dramatizes stories or parts of stories
- Makes predictions based on illustrations or portions of stories
- Listens attentively to books the teacher reads in class
- Continues to progress in segmenting words into syllables; 90 percent of children can count the number of syllables in a word
- Can identify words as beginning with the same sound
- Given a few words, can pick out the word with a different beginning sound
- Understands that spoken words consist of a sequence of phonemes
- Can produce the beginning sound in a word (when asked to say the first sound of the word "mat," he answers, "*mmmm*")
- Counts the number of phonemes in a small word; when asked to count the sounds he hears in "me," he finds two (accomplished by 70 to 80 percent of children)
- Blends individual sounds of phonemes together to make a word (when asked what word the sound *shhh* and *oooo* make, he answers "shoe")

End of Kindergarten Accomplishments (Ages Five and a Half to Six): Print
- Recognizes and names all the letters of the alphabet
- Knows the sounds of almost all the letters of the alphabet
- Can write most letters and some words when they are dictated
- Understands that the sequence of letters within a written word represents the sequence of sounds heard in the spoken word
- Begins to decode simple words
- Recognizes a growing number of common words by sight ("I," "you," "my," "are," "is," "the")
- Uses invented spelling, such as writing "krr" for "car"
- Writes many uppercase and lowercase letters
- Writes his or her own name (first and last) and the names of family members or pets
- Writes (unconventionally) to express his own ideas

Chapter 11

Ready or Not, Here I Come

Overheard after the first day of school:
FATHER: Well, son, how do you like going to school?
SON: I like the going and coming;, it's the part in the middle I don't like.

Putting a child on the bus for the first day of kindergarten is a momentous occasion. It formally marks the end of one era and the beginning of another. While the first day of preschool is a pretty big deal, parents still feel they have a sense of total control over their child's destiny. However, once the child climbs on that big yellow bus, a large part of control over the child's life shifts to the huge bureaucracy that is the American educational system. For better or worse, the teacher, the classmates, and the school environment take on great influence over most of his waking hours.

For most children, the transition is a seamless shift from the world of preschool or day care to the world of elementary school, and many await with eagerness the chance to hop on that bus or to walk into that school building. For some, there is trepidation, but with some coaxing and reassurance, they are willing to give it a go. For an unfortunate few, the experience seems just too traumatic to cope with, and they fight and scream as though their very lives were about to end. And in some ways, it does—at least, life as they once knew it. What makes some children seem so ready and eager to go to school and others desperate to head back out the door?

Photo: SW Productions / Brand X Pictures / Getty Images

Kindergarten Readiness

Over the years, educational experts, developmental psychologists, policymakers, and administrators have wrestled with the problem of determining when children are ready for kindergarten. Much has been made about *when* a child should enter school. While each state can set its own cutoff date for the age a child must be in order to enter school, most require that a child be five years old by September of the year of school entry. However, school is not usually compulsory until age six (in twenty states) or seven (in twenty-two states). In the 1970s and 1980s, attention was brought to the issue of developmental age. Some child psychologists, such as those at the Gesell Institute—a well-known center specializing in school readiness—strongly advocated assessing children for developmental levels prior to school entry. They made the claim that remedial ranks, that is, children requiring special help, could be cut by 50 percent if schools would just allow children to enter the appropriate grade when they were developmentally ready. They recommended looking at readiness in different areas, such as intellectual functioning, social development, and gross- and fine-motor development, stressing that while a child might be intellectually superior, he might be emotionally immature and hence unready to enter and be successful in kindergarten. They pointed out the unfair effect of using a single arbitrary cutoff date. A girl who just missed the cutoff will enter kindergarten when she is almost six. A boy who just made the cutoff date will be entering kindergarten when he is five or, in some cases, even late four. Based on the known tendency of girls to generally be ahead of boys in development at this age, a huge discrepancy is created in the functioning levels of children in a given class. An increasing number of parents (9 or 10 percent according to research surveys) choose to hold back their child, especially if it's a boy with a birthday very close to the cutoff date. But the effect of this in a particular school is to raise the average age of kindergartners, making it an even tougher decision for those parents who have questions about their own child's readiness. The parent of a younger boy with known weaknesses in language, from a highly affluent, upwardly mobile community, said, "I'm afraid to send him this year even though he's old enough. In our community, most parents deliberately wait until their child is six, hoping that will increase the child's chance for being at the top of the class."

What About Testing for Readiness?

Many school districts screen children prior to entry, assessing their readiness for school entry. While this information can be useful in planning for the child's needs, experts argue that it should not be used as a basis for deterring parents from sending their child to kindergarten. The very children who would be turned away are the ones who seem to benefit the most from their first year in school, according to studies of these children.

Does Delaying Entry Increase Chances for Success?

There is little evidence to suggest that older children do better in kindergarten, according to the position statement of the National Association for the Education of Young Children on school readiness. Some studies have shown that there is a small advantage in being relatively older than classmates, but this diminishes or disappears by the upper elementary grades, according to a comprehensive review of existing research. The position statement developed by the National Association of Early Childhood Specialists in State Departments of Education states, "The 'gift of time' that many parents have been persuaded to give children by delaying school entry can result instead in denying them opportunities for cognitive growth through social interaction with the their age-mates."

Ready for What?

More recently, some child development experts have raised concern about the effects of later school entry dates, a growing trend nationwide. With greater emphasis being placed on standardized testing in elementary grades, they fear there will be pressure filtering downward, with increasing demands placed on children in kindergarten. The justification for this added pressure is that children entering kindergarten now are older and smarter, given all the preschool and television they are exposed to. Well-meaning, overly zealous parents demanding that higher academic skills be taught earlier may inadvertently contribute to an increase in paper-and-pencil types of tasks and an inappropriately large amount of time spent doing desk work. As one expert put it, "Clearly all children at all ages are 'ready to learn.' The meaningful question is not *whether* a child is ready to learn, but rather *what* a child is ready to learn."

Ask Not

Some experts are now suggesting that the question "Is my child ready for school?" be reversed. They suggest that we should ask not whether the children are ready for school, but whether the school is ready for the children. Child educators Kelly Maxwell and Richard Clifford say that "school readiness involves more than just children. School readiness, in the broadest sense, is about children, families, early environments, schools, and communities. Children are not innately *ready* or *not ready* for school." Advocates of delaying school entry focus on the child's readiness for the "program." Inherent in this philosophy is the idea that a curriculum is fixed and that children must fit into it. Deborah Stipek, in an article published by the Society for Research in Child Development, argues that a better approach is to "adapt the curriculum to the developmental levels of children who enter kindergarten, whatever their cognitive and social skills." She states that "we would do a much greater service to children if we focused more on making school ready for children than on making children ready for school."

To Send or Not to Send

The decision to delay a child's entry into school is ultimately the parents' choice. There may be some legitimate arguments supporting delayed school entry, but in general, it is probably better to err on the side of sending them despite reservations. The child may surprise you and rise to the occasion, doing much better than expected. Certainly, if there are concerns about learning issues, you will want to be in close communication with the classroom teacher and find out about any difficulties sooner rather than later. Be involved and become informed about all aspects of your child's curriculum. Find out what reading-readiness skills are taught directly and how your child is handling them. Repeating kindergarten may be an option if you and the teacher both feel it would help. However, if there are specific learning issues, these may not be resolved with another year in kindergarten.

Early Identification of Language-Based Learning Disabilities

Julie, a second grader, used to enjoy going to school. In preschool and kindergarten, she was bubbly and had lots of playmates. Then in first grade, she began to complain of stomach pains in the morning and frequently requested staying home from school. She seemed anxious and withdrawn. Her teacher described her as quiet and shy, and said she "tries hard" to complete her work. Learning to read had been a slow process, and Julie began to avoid situations in which she had to read out loud. As a toddler, she had enjoyed being read to, but by the end of first grade, she was avoiding books altogether. Her parents, concerned that she wasn't picking up on reading skills, requested that she be tested. She was, but her scores, the parents were told, weren't low enough to warrant extra help—some children just took longer to learn to read than others. By the end of second grade, however, things were getting worse. Her parents took her to a reading specialist, who diagnosed her as being dyslexic. With the help of a private tutor, she began to make solid progress in reading but was still below grade level and struggled to keep up with the reading and writing activities in her classroom.

Traditionally, school districts have followed this type of "wait till they fail" policy. Students have had to demonstrate a significant discrepancy between potential (measured via IQ testing) and achievement (ability to perform in reading, spelling, and math) before special help could be given. The problem with this policy is that valuable time in the early primary grades can be wasted, and, according to Sally Shaywitz in *Overcoming Dyslexia,* a "rich get richer, and poor get poorer" process sets in. Poor readers tend to read much less often, whereas good readers tend to read frequently. A study of elementary students found that poor readers read, on average, less than one minute each day, exposing them to approximately eight thousand words a year. Top readers, on the other hand, averaged more than twenty minutes a day, resulting in an average of 1.8 million words a year. At this rate, it would take a poor reader a whole year to read what a good reader would read in two days. This creates huge differences in vocabulary acquisition, since books use more sophisticated words than conversational speech. Many schools are now aggressively screening for learning difficulties during the kindergarten year, but the tests are so general that they do not identify children who are at risk for reading failure. However, screening methods are continuing to improve, and there are now simple time- and cost-effective screening methods available.

The following checklist was developed by Hugh Catts, a professor at the University of Kansas and an expert in the area of language-based learning disabilities. It is intended for use with children at the *end of kindergarten or beginning of first grade.* A child who exhibits many of the following characteristics should be referred for more in-depth evaluation by a language and learning specialist.

[Reprinted with permission from the American Speech-Language-Hearing Association]:

Speech Sound Awareness

- Doesn't understand and enjoy rhymes
- Doesn't easily recognize that words may begin with the same sound
- Has difficulty counting the syllables in spoken words
- Has problem clapping hands or tapping feet in rhythm with songs and/ or rhymes
- Demonstrates problems learning sound-letter correspondences

Word Retrieval

- Has difficulty retrieving a specific word (for example, calls a sheep a "goat" or says "you know, a woolly animal")
- Shows poor memory for classmates' names
- Speech is hesitant, filled with pauses or vocalizations (for example, "um," "you know")
- Frequently uses words lacking specificity (for example, "stuff," "thing," "what you call it")
- Has a problem remembering/retrieving verbal sequences (for example, days of the week, alphabet)

Verbal Memory

- Has difficulty remembering instructions or directions
- Shows problems learning names of people or places
- Has difficulty remembering the words to songs or poems
- Has problems learning a second language

Speech Production/Perception

- Has problems saying common words with difficult sound patterns (for example, "animal," "cinnamon," "specific")
- Mishears and subsequently mispronounces words or names
- Confuses a similar-sounding word with another word (for example, saying "The Entire State Building is in New York")
- Combines sound patterns of similar words (for example, saying "escavator" for "escalator")
- Shows frequent slips of the tongue (for example, saying "brue blush" for "blue brush")
- Has difficulty with tongue twisters (for example, "She sells seashells")

Comprehension

- Only responds to part of a multiple-element request or instruction
- Requests multiple repetitions of instructions/directions with little improvement in comprehension
- Relies too much on context to understand what is said
- Has difficulty understanding questions
- Fails to understand age-appropriate stories
- Has difficulty making inferences, predicting outcomes, drawing conclusions
- Lacks understanding of spatial terms, such as left-right, front-back

Expressive Language

- Talks in short sentences
- Makes errors in grammar (for example, "he goed to the store" or "me want that")
- Lacks variety in vocabulary (for example, uses "good" to mean happy, kind, polite)
- Has difficulty giving directions or explanations (for example, may show multiple revisions or dead ends)
- Relates stories or events in a disorganized or incomplete manner
- May have much to say but provides little specific detail
- Has difficulty with the rules of conversation, such as turn taking, staying on topic, indicating when he/she does not understand

Dyslexia: What We Know So Far

Reading is a language-based skill. Therefore, any deficits in the development of spoken language can have a negative effect on the process of learning to read. Children with weaknesses in language skills at the preschool level have a greater risk of developing dyslexia, and the reverse is also true—many children with dyslexia have concomitant language problems.

What exactly is dyslexia? Old stereotypes of children who see words backward and confuse *b*'s and *d*'s have given way to a newer and more complete understanding of this disorder. The term "dyslexia" is used to describe unexpected and significant difficulties in learning to read in the presence of normal intelligence. According to Sally Shaywitz, a leading expert on the disorder, it affects approximately one in every five children, or about ten million children in the United States alone. The following is a list of known facts she provides in her book *Overcoming Dyslexia:*

- There is a genetic predisposition for dyslexia. Though there is no single isolated gene, the disorder tends to run in families and is probably the result of several interacting genes.

- One fourth to one half of the children born to a dyslexic parent will also be dyslexic.
- Dyslexia is unrelated to intelligence; many students with dyslexia are extremely bright.
- A primary cause appears to be differences in the brain that create difficulty with the ability to connect the sounds in spoken language to their written letter counterparts.
- Children with dyslexia can be taught to read with proper instruction.
- While many children with dyslexia go on to successfully complete college and have productive careers, they will have persisting weaknesses in reading fluency.
- The earlier the diagnosis, the better. A child who is not identified until third or fourth grade will be at a great disadvantage, because at this point, the curriculum shifts from learning to read to reading to learn.

It has only been fairly recently that medical technology, such as functional magnetic resonance imaging, has provided concrete and visual proof of the differences in the way the brain of a person with dyslexia learns to read. The exciting corollary is that direct and systematic instruction in phonemic awareness and phonological processing (phonics types of skills) have produced observable differences in these brain images. Why, then, is it that most children are currently still not diagnosed until they are in the third grade? The answer is that in the past, we have lacked adequate assessment tools to accurately predict which children will have this problem. As more research is gathered, this is changing, and there are now fairly accurate, cost-effective assessment tests that can be administered to five-year-olds.

Early Clues

The hallmark feature of dyslexia in young children is a specific weakness in dealing with the sounds of letters and words, despite solid intellectual and reasoning ability. This weakness in dealing with the sounds of letters and words, or phonologic weakness, can be manifested by the following, according to Shaywitz:

- A delay in the onset of speaking, usually a modest one and often dismissed as "late talking runs in the family"
- Difficulties in pronunciation: leaving out syllables, mixing up the sounds in words
- Insensitivity to rhyme
- Word-retrieval difficulties
- Difficulty learning the names of alphabet letters and the sounds they make

Will My Kindergartner Have Trouble Learning to Read?

Shaywitz offers a checklist of the skills a child should have by the end of kindergarten. The child should have no difficulty learning to read if he

- Knows that spoken words come apart and that letters represent these sounds
- Easily names the letters of the alphabet, both uppercase and lowercase
- Writes the letters of the alphabet
- Is beginning to learn about letter-sound matches
- Is beginning to decode simple words
- Is beginning to recognize some common sight words
- Uses invented spellings
- Knows about print conventions—reading from left to right, from the top of the page to the bottom
- Has a growing vocabulary
- Looks forward to reading

Is There Anything That Can Be Done?

Certainly a child with a history of language delay or weakness or a child with a parent who has dyslexia should be carefully monitored for signs of phonologic weakness. At ages five to six, high-risk children can be given screening tests that assess the skills listed above. Shaywitz suggests that since children enter kindergarten with such a wide range of previous exposure, it is helpful to wait at least half a year before conducting a general screening to allow children access to some instruction. There are a few good sources for such screening tests, including:

- Texas Education Agency: Primary Reading Inventory (TPRI) *www.tpri.org*
- University of Virginia: Phonological Awareness Literacy Screening (PALS) *http://curry.edschool.virginia.edu/go/pals/*
- University of Oregon: Dynamic Indicators of Basic Early Literacy Skills (DIBELS) *http://dibels.uoregon.edu.skills*

Where to Find Help If You Suspect a Problem

Perhaps your two-year-old is not talking yet or is saying only a few words. Maybe your three-year-old uses some language but has no interest in conversing or interacting and seems not to be listening much of the time. Perhaps your four-year-old's speech is so hard to understand that his peers select other playmates. Perhaps your preschooler is having difficulty behaving in nursery school and has no interest in hearing a story and won't sit still during circle or story time. Or maybe everything seemed fine in preschool, but your kindergartner lacks several skills on the checklist for prereading skills. Part of you wants to wait and see if the problem will resolve itself, but that is not the best course to take. If you suspect a problem, *don't wait*. Get it checked out. At best, you will find out that you have been worrying unnecessarily. So what if someone thinks you're an overanxious parent. And if it should turn out that your child does have weaknesses that need intervention, help is available (if your child qualifies). And receiving help early on can make a huge difference later, when the child moves through the school system. An excellent resource for parents of children with language delays is *The Late Talker* by Marilyn C. Agin, Lisa F. Geng, and Malcolm J. Nicholl.

Usually, your first guide in determining whether or not your child has a problem is the pediatrician. If the pediatrician tells you not to worry and that everything will be fine, that may well be the case, but it might be good to get a second opinion. You are allowed to question the opinion of a doctor! You don't need a referral from a pediatrician to have your child's language skills screened or evaluated. An excellent person to speak with is the director of your child's day-care or nursery school. Talk about your concerns and ask for advice. Speech-language pathologists (SLPs) are trained to diagnose and treat language problems. Arrange for a consultation, screening, or complete diagnostic evaluation at your local speech and hearing center, often located in a large hospital, or with a private SLP. Make sure the person you are seeing is licensed and certified by the American Speech-Language-Hearing Association (ASHA). A list of certified professionals in your area is accessible on the ASHA Web site at *www.ASHA.org*.

Whom Do I Contact?

This will vary, depending on the age of your child.

- Birth to age three, contact your pediatrician, the local department of health, or an SLP
- Ages three to five, contact your pediatrician, the local school district (ask for the committee on preschool special education), or an SLP
- Ages five and up, if your child is in school, talk with your child's teacher first to express your concerns and get her opinion. If you feel it is necessary, formally request the school district, preferably in writing, that your child be screened or evaluated, and describe your reasons. Your state education department can provide you with literature regarding your rights as a parent.

For a list of other organizations and sources of help, see Appendix B. You know your child best and are your child's best advocate. Follow your instincts. If you feel your child needs help, *get involved!*

Glossary

Auditory processing: The ability to hear, discriminate, and perceive spoken language so as to derive the meaning of its content.

Babbling: The sounds and sound combinations produced by infants before they produce real words.

Contingent response: A response on the part of an adult to the sounds or words produced by an infant or young child that immediately follows and is directly related to the child's utterance.

Cooing: Open vowels, such as *oooh* or *ahhh,* that are produced by infants prior to babbling.

Dyslexia: A specific impairment in learning to read.

Expressive language: Expressive language is what is spoken—language that is expressed. When your child responds, "Okay, but I'll do it in a minute because I'm busy now," she is using expressive language—the ability to speak and use language in talking. (And she is probably using language she has heard you say to her!)

Invented spelling: Written letters and letter combinations that a child produces in early attempts to write down words, prior to formal knowledge of spelling.

Jargon: Strings of sounds that are babbled with sentencelike stress and intonation patterns.

Metalinguistics: Labeling and/or describing knowledge about language; the ability to think and talk about one's language.

Morphology: This refers to the individual words and word parts, such as plurals and past tense *-ed* (jump*ed*), that are used to help make what we are saying more specific. A child who says "I goed to my grandma's house" is showing that he knows that the past tense morpheme *-ed* goes at the end of a word to denote past tense but has not yet refined the rule to leave off the ending in irregular verbs.

Object permanence: The understanding that objects continue to exist even though they may be out of view, usually gained during the latter part of the first year.

Oral-motor development: "Oral-motor" refers to the structure and movements of parts of the mouth, including the lips, tongue, and jaw. There is an orderly development that occurs for both feeding and speech. The same muscles that enable the tongue, jaw, and lips to complete chewing and swallowing movements are the ones that enable production of speech sounds.

Otitis media: Infection of the middle ear.

Phoneme: A speech sound that can indicate a difference in meaning. In English, *p* and *b* are phonemes, because when one is substituted for the other, the meaning of a word changes, for example, "pat" versus "bat." When the young child says "The wed wabbit was wunning" instead of "The red rabbit was running," we can say that he has not yet acquired the *r* phoneme, or that he substitutes a *w* phoneme for an *r* phoneme."

Phonology: The sounds that make up a language and the rules for their combination and use. Every language has a specific and unique set of sounds— both consonants and vowels—that make up the phonemes of that language.

Pragmatics: The rules for using language to interact with other people, such as knowing how to stay on a topic, change the topic, take turns talking, and use polite forms in appropriate situations. When a five-year-old sees a plate of cookies and says, "I'm really hungry, and I love cookies," he is showing that he knows how to be more indirect (and more polite) in making requests.

Receptive language: The hearing of spoken words and the ability to understand what they mean. When a three-year-old is told to go upstairs and get her shoes and socks and she does it, she has used receptive-language skills. (And if she doesn't do it, it doesn't necessarily mean that she has a problem with receptive language!)

Semantics: The meaning system of a language—understanding and using words and concepts. When your child says "I want the bigger one," he is showing that he understands the semantic concept of size and can use the correct word to express that concept.

Syntax: The system of rules in a language by which sentences are formed; the connecting of words in the proper order to create grammatically correct forms, such as declarative, interrogative and imperative sentences. When a child asks "Why he's going?" instead of "Why is he going?" we can see that he has not yet acquired the syntactic rule that word order is reversed when asking questions.

Appendix A

Language Activities for Preschool (LAP)

Expressive Language Activities

Hide-and-Tell. Give each child a paper bag or a box. Help them find an object in the classroom without others watching and hide it in their bag or box. Or you can have each child can bring something from home and hide it. Each child gets a turn to give clues about what's in his or her bag: "It's something you cut with It's made of metal." The child gets to call on other children, who may make a guess or ask further questions. This continues until someone guesses what the object is.

Six-Million-Dollar Pyramid. This is based on an old TV show. A set of cards is selected. These can be pictures of items within a single category group or from several categories. Review the names of the pictured items. One person is the guesser; the other, the teller of the clues. The teller picks up a card and starts describing it, giving the category name and/or features—for example, "It's an animal. It lives in the jungle. It roars." The guesser tries to guess the item. Once it is guessed, the card is discarded, and the next card is described in similar fashion. The goal is to successfully describe and name all of the items. Then the roles can be switched, so that the teller becomes the guesser. To make the game more exciting, a sand timer or stopwatch can be used to add time pressure. (Be aware that this may penalize children who take a longer time to retrieve words and therefore may not be a good choice.) To use a timer in a less competitive way, have each pair of children be a team that tries to beat their previous time.

Make It Longer. Seat children in a semicircle around a table. Put two blocks, poker chips, or colored shapes on the table. Start by saying a kernel sentence, one consisting of just a subject and a verb, such as "He walked," touching a token for each word as it is spoken. Have the children repeat the two words together out loud as you point to each token. Then say, "Let's make it longer. *Where* did he walk?" Have the children come up with a phrase—for example, "to the store." Then put additional tokens on the table, and repeat the longer sentence with the children in unison as you point to each of the five tokens. Next say, "Let's make it even longer! *When* did he walk to the store?" Talk about some possible answers: "Maybe he walked to the store yesterday; or maybe he walked to the store on Saturday." Select a child to give an appropriate answer, then add the additional tokens and repeat the sentence again. Continue by asking, "*Why* did he go to the store? To get some milk? To get some candy?" Select an appropriate answer, and place the necessary tokens. Then repeat the whole sentence. Once the sentence is very long, have the children help count the number of words in that sentence and drop the blocks or other tokens into a container. Small food tokens can be used to make this a fun snack-time activity. Talk about how "long" the sentence was. Then start a new kernel sentence. Children will enjoy trying to top the previous length by making an even longer sentence.

Who Did What? Where? Collect four small flower pots or heavy cups. Label each with one of the following words: "who," "did," "what," "where." Using craft sticks, glue pictures of items on the sticks to represent examples of each of the above. For example, the "who" sticks might have pictures of a clown, a mom, a dad, a baby, or a policeman. The "did" sticks would have pictures of actions. Try to use actions that can be performed on objects, such as "kicked," "kissed," "threw," "hid," "dropped," or "took." "What" sticks would have pictures of objects, and "where" sticks, pictures of places: a school, a park, a store, or a living room. The children take one stick from each of the pots or cups and try to make a sentence. They will have fun making up nonsensical sentences, such as "The clown hid the umbrella under the rug." These can be extended by adding answers to "why?"

What's the Story? Stories, Stories, and More Stories

Sequence-Picture Stories. Use large picture-sequence cards. Place each card on a table or in a pocket chart, and have the children generate part of a story. Continue until all the cards have been placed. Have one child tell the whole story. Another way is to pass out the cards. Tell the story again, and have the child with that card come up and place the card in the chart. Or scramble the cards, and have the children help each other to place them in the right order. Point out incorrect sequences by saying, "Do you think he put on his coat *before* he ate breakfast? Or *after* breakfast?"

This activity lends itself nicely to planning a cooking activity. Create a picture for each direction provided in a recipe. Review the sequence before the cooking activity and then again after; children can take turns telling, in order, "all the things we did."

Using digital photographs of the children performing a sequence is always a fun way to engage them in a sequencing activity. Take pictures of the sequence of a daily classroom routine or a field trip. Using the computer, enlarge each picture to create personalized sequence stories for the classroom.

Magical Storyland. Create a special area of the room, designated as storyland, in which imaginary things take place and are told about. You might have a large pretend tree, some grass carpet, and maybe some large clouds up on the wall. Keep a large trunk or footlocker—or a small clothes rack with hangers—filled with props, hats, and other dress-up clothes. You might also want a tape recorder or CD player for playing music or recorded stories.

Story Center. Tape-record a story of the week, and provide a few copies of the story itself for children to look at together while listening. Have a flannel board set up so children can retell the story on their own.

Group Story. Use a cassette recorder. With the children seated in a circle on the floor, tape-record a one-sentence story starter. Have each child take a turn and create the next sentence to the story, tape-recording as you go around the group. At the end, play back the tape to hear the whole story. Children really enjoy hearing themselves on tape. If the story is good, let each child draw a picture to go with his or her sentence. Then punch holes in the pages and connect with rings to make a class booklet. Modification: Use a simple repetitive story, such as Laura Joffe Numeroff's *If You Give a Mouse a Cookie,* and let each child record his or her own sentence and draw a corresponding picture.

Clothesline Story. Cut apart pages of a well-known picture-book story. As you tell each part of the story, hang the page on the line with a clothespin. Have the children retell the story at the end. The clothesline and pins can be set up in the storyland area for children to try on their own.

Participatory Stories. When reading a story out loud, assign a sound to be made by a particular child each time he hears a certain word. A story that has farm animals, such as *The Little Red Hen,* works well. Assign various animal parts to the children, and have them make the corresponding sound each time their character is mentioned.

Story Boxes. Using shoeboxes or small plastic storage boxes, create kits, placing small props, felt-board characters, and a copy of a storybook in each box. Demonstrate how to reenact the story using the props.

Hey, We're on TV! Activities for Use with a Video Camcorder

Wild Kingdom. Each child selects a stuffed or toy animal that might be seen on a safari or in a rain forest or jungle. Have the child practice telling about the animal—what its features are, what it eats, and so forth. Use a video camcorder to interview each child about his animal. Play back the results for the entire class to watch and enjoy.

Evening News. Have children take turns as the designated newscaster. Videotape each child narrating a report, such as the following:

- "On the Playground." A child describes what playmates are doing.
- "A Tour of Our School." Walk around the school, letting children take turns narrating about each area. Plan an interview with some of the staff, such as the principal, secretary, custodian, or kitchen workers.
- "A Tour of Our Classroom." This is a great for the beginning of the year, which can be played for back-to-school night for parents.

Role Playing

Role playing around a weekly theme helps make stories come alive and stimulates pretend play and dialogue. Create an area designated for role playing based on the latest theme. For example, after reading about a visit to the doctor or a hospital stay, arrange various props in a certain area, including a doctor's kit, Band-Aids, dolls, beds, face masks, and white coats and create a related scenario, such as a mother calling the doctor to make an appointment. Other themes could include an airport, post office, campground, grocery store, McDonald's, and school. Here are some examples.

Officer, My Child Is Lost! While the rest of the class watches, one child plays a police officer and another pretends to be the parent of a "missing" child. Provide a police hat (purchased at a uniform shop or from a toy catalogue), a badge, and a dark blue shirt for the police officer. The parent must call the police and describe her child. Choose one child to be described as the missing child. The police officer will look over the group and pick out the child that fits the description, bring this child to the parent, and say, "Is this your child?"

Call the Vet/My Puppy Is Sick. Have each child bring in a stuffed or toy animal in a shoebox serving as the bed. Cut up an old white sheet to serve as blankets for the beds. Obtain a doctor's kit with a stethoscope, a thermometer, and a toy hypodermic needle. Use an old white shirt for a lab coat. Arrange the empty shoeboxes in rows to simulate a hospital ward. Have each child call on a toy phone to describe the symptoms and to arrange an appointment for his sick pet. Let children take turns being the vet (you may also have a vet's assistant), who listens to the complaints and treats the animal with an overnight stay in a shoebox bed.

Have a Seat—the Doctor Will Be Right With You. The scenario is basically the same as the one above, but instead of pets, the patients are dolls or teddy bears brought in from home. Set up a waiting-room area with small chairs and magazines. Have a child, playing a nurse or receptionist, do the intake by taking down the name, address, and complaint of each pretend patient or patient's parent. An examination table can be set up using an overturned storage crate or box covered with a white sheet. A hospital can also be simulated by using the shoe boxes described above. Makeshift medical supplies can be collected, such as Band-Aids, gauze, elastic braces, and cotton swabs. An operating room can be created, and a small rolling cart can be used as a gurney. Have the children take turns phoning the doctor's office or hospital for an appointment and describing the problem.

Houston, We Have a Problem! Simulations of space exploration are always met with enthusiasm. An astronaut's costume can be created using a football helmet and a large-size snow suit. Simulate an air tank by using a backpack and length of old vacuum hose attached to the back of the helmet. Create a spacecraft by using a child's car seat with a seat belt, surrounded by a large cylinder made out of poster board or a cut-up and reshaped refrigerator box. Inexpensive walkie-talkies enable the astronaut to communicate with ground control. Space snacks can be created by using juice pouches and zippered food-storage bags. A corner of the classroom can be set up as the destination planet. Drape a large curtain or bedspread over the area to be explored, and place various rocks or other objects on it. The space traveler must report back to ground control about the findings.

May I Take Your Order Please? A few T-shirts or vests and makeshift caps or paper headbands, a table, and some fake food will be enough to get started taking orders and serving up some fast food. Additional props: small trays, paper plates and cups, straws, plastic utensils, and fake food made from Play-Doh or magazine pictures cut out and glued onto heavy paper. A cash register and some play money will complete the scene. If three different size cups can be found, this can be a good way to practice the concepts of small, medium, and large. With some modification, the fast-food restaurant can be turned into an ice-cream shop, using different-color Play Doh, miniature scoops, and paper plate bowls. Make cones out of tan construction paper by rolling pieces of paper into cone shapes and stapling the edges together.

You may also decide to create a sit-down restaurant, complete with tables and chairs, menus, and small pads and pencils for taking orders. Waitstaff uniforms can be made using smocks, vests, scarves, or aprons. Make sure there are plenty of wallets and fake money in order to pay the bill and leave a tip!

Mail Call! This is a fun activity around Valentine's Day, though it works anytime. Have a business-size envelope with each child's name written in large, colorful letters. (If desired, you can also write the child's real address on the envelope.) Give each child an envelope with another child's name on it, and have him create a message to be placed in the envelope, such as a note dictated to and written down by the teacher or a self-created drawing decorated with stickers or stamps. Have the child place a stamp or sticker on the envelope in order to mail it. Create a mailbox by covering a container or box with blue and white paper and cut a slot through which the letters can be dropped inside the box. Create a mail carrier's costume using a blue shirt or jacket, and a shoulder bag. Have the mail carrier take the envelopes out of the mailbox, stamp each envelope as a postmark, and place all the envelopes in the bag. Have the mailman deliver each letter to the appropriate child, with help as needed in reading the names.

Will That Be Cash or Credit? Create a small store—grocery, candy store, bakery, toy store—by collecting the appropriate objects. Make small shopping baskets using shoeboxes, with strips of heavy poster paper fastened on each side of the box to serve as handles. Set up a checkout area with a toy cash register and with paper or plastic bags to place the purchased objects in. Model the dialogue, and set up the situation so that the shopper needs to ask for various items. You can use fake money, with small purses and wallets provided to the shoppers. Many toy cash registers come with small plastic credit cards, or you can make your own by using cardboard simulations.

Don't Pet the Alligators: A Day at the Zoo. Have each child bring in a box with a plastic or stuffed animal suitable for a zoo. Glue or staple strips of paper on the open side of the boxes to simulate the bars of a cage, or tie several strings around the box. Let the children take turns describing their animals' features and habits. For a more elaborate version, use a small cart or wagon in which the zookeeper can place all the necessary pretend food items—leaves, berries, fish, meat, hay, and the like. Let children take turns being the zookeeper.

How Much Is That Doggie in the Window? A Trip to the Pet Store. This is the same idea as above, but the animals would be dogs, cats, mice, snakes, birds, and other pet-store animals. Allow the children to take turns being the pet-store worker, describing the animals and answering questions, and the consumers, shopping for a new pet. Have the shoppers ask questions about the habits, care, and feeding of the animal(s) they are interested in.

Fasten Your Seat Belts: Airport. Everyone loves to go on a trip. Have two double rows of chairs to simulate the seating on an airplane. This is a great way to practice numbers and letters if you tape row numbers and seat letters on the chairs. Use old belts as seat belts. Have uniforms for the pilot and co-pilot (hat and blue shirt) and stewardesses (apron or scarf as sash), pretend food, a small cart, and baggage (small suitcases).

Teddy-Bear Picnic. Have the children each bring in their favorite teddy bear. Lay out blankets and have a teddy-bear picnic at snack time. Have each child tell about her bear—the name, where it came from, why she likes it, and so forth. If possible, take a photo of each child and her bear, and use the computer to record her dictated sentences about her bear. Place all the pages in a classroom Teddy-Bear Book. Tape-record each child's description on a cassette tape for play-along.

Talent Show. Every child is proud of *something* he can do, even if it's just hop on one foot, do a somersault, sing a favorite song, make a silly face, display a collection from home, demonstrate a karate kick, or play a few notes on an instrument. This one is fun to videotape for later playback.

Under the Big Top. Everybody loves the circus, and there is a role for just about everyone, including the circus master (hat and jacket), clown (pajamas and makeup), acrobats (tights and/or tutus), and animal trainers (hula hoop to hold). Role playing around this theme will require supervision if there is a group. A rope can be stretched out on the floor to simulate walking the high wire, and stuffed animals can be made to jump through the hoop. Provide a handheld toy microphone for the circus master. If adults are available, one can shine a spotlight on each act. Another can provide a makeshift elephant ride! Peanuts, regular popcorn, and Cracker Jack popcorn are optional! A trip to a real circus is preferable, and here are a few circus books: *Circus! A Pop-Up Adventure* by Meg Davenport and Lisa V. Werenk, *The Circus Alphabet* by Linda Bronson, *Olivia Saves the Circus* by Ian Falconer, and *Mirette on the High Wire* by Emily Arnold McCully. There are many others that your librarian will be happy to show you.

Receptive Language (Listening) Activities

Tick Tock, Find the Clock. A designated child is asked to step out of the room for a moment. A ticking clock (kitchen timers work well) is hidden somewhere in the room by another child. The first child reenters and begins roaming the room, listening for the ticking clock. Classmates will call out "Getting warmer" or "Getting colder" as the person moves closer or farther from the clock.

Knock, Knock, Who's There? Record each child describing himself or herself without giving his or her name. During group circle time, play back the tape, beginning each child's segment by making a knocking sound and then asking, "Who's there?" Play the tape segment and have the class guess whose voice it is. This activity can be nicely adapted to a classroom book by creating a separate page for each child, on which the corresponding child's photo can be placed, one at a time, as the words are played back on the tape.

Copycat Clapping Game. This game requires listening for a number of taps or claps, ranging from one to four. Choose a leader who taps on a drum or claps her hands one to four times. She calls on another child to replicate the number of claps or taps. If that child is correct, he becomes the leader.

Treasure Hunt: Following Directions With Colors and Shapes. Using colored felt, foam sheets, oilcloth, or construction paper, make a set of colored shapes of various sizes—for example, small and large circles, squares, rectangles, and triangles. Place them on the floor to form a trail from one side of the room to the other. Make up instruction cards, such as "Go three steps forward," "Go to the next square [or circle or triangle]," and "Go to a large [small], blue [red or green] shape." If the player gets to the other end of the trail by following the instructions correctly, he receives a small treasure (sticker, snack item, gold chocolate coin). A simpler version of this game is floor-size Candy Land. Make the trail using square pieces of colored paper in the same shades as the game cards. Create candy spaces using white paper on which the candies are drawn. Have one person be the caller who draws a card and tells which person to move to which color. If children get a candy that requires them to go very far back, I usually allow them to say "No, thank you" and stay where they are, since this can be frustrating.

Naming and Categorization (Semantic) Skills

Basic Categories Guessing Game. Using a commercially available or homemade set of picture cards containing items from several categories, help the children name and place items from about five categories in rows, with each row containing a single category. Children take turns making others guess items by saying, "I'm thinking of a food. It is round and has a hole in the middle," and such. Other children raise their hands if they think they know the answer, and the first child calls on a classmate to guess the answer. If the guess is correct, it becomes that child's turn to give the next set of clues.

Guess My Feature. Using the same set of cards as in the above activity, place a hula hoop on a table or create a circle made of yarn. Have one child select a card and place it within the hoop or circle. Then have the next child pick a card with some feature in common with the first. It may be the general category, such as animals, or it may be a physical aspect of the item, such as "round" or "has four legs." The third child has to guess the feature that the first two cards have in common. If he is correct, it becomes his turn next. Play continues until all cards with that feature have been found. This activity will need some demonstrating by the teacher first.

Hoop the Group. Use the hula hoop or yarn circle and the cards, as described above. The cards are placed faceup on the table and mixed up. The teacher calls out a category name, and children take turns finding and naming all the items in that category as they place them inside the hoop.

Opposites. Use commercially available or homemade opposite cards. Sort them into two piles. One pile will be given to the caller; the rest are dealt out to the children in the group. The caller draws a picture from his pile and names the picture. The child holding the opposite must identify it, and if he does, he gets to keep the pair. Play continues until all the cards have been matched.

Word Power Tower. Each child is given several small cube-shaped blocks and told to build a tower of words. In order to place a block on the tower, the child must think of a word in the category chosen for that tower. For example, if the selected category is animals, each child, in turn, may place a block on the tower as he says the name of an animal. Play continues until no one can think of any more animals. The last person to think of an animal gets to knock the tower down and name a new category to begin another tower. This game can also be used to have children think of rhyming words or words that begin with a designated sound.

Activities for Developing Reading Readiness (Phonemic Awareness)

There are several good source books and materials available commercially. Here are a few titles and their publishers: *Earobics* (Cognitive Concepts), *Ladders to Literacy* (Brookes Publishing Company), *Phonemic Awareness in Young Children: A Classroom Curriculum* (Brookes Publishing Company), *The Sounds Abound Program: Teaching Phonological Awareness in the Classroom* (LinguiSystems), and *Phonological Awareness Board Games* (Pro-Ed).

Rhyming

Name Rhyming Game. Pick a letter sound, for example *b*. Go around the circle of children and create a rhyme with each child's name using that sound, for instance, Matthew Batthew or Jennifer Bennifer. This can be used when children are lining up: "If your name rhymes with Bennifer, you may get on line."

Rhyming Object Sort. Collect a set of rhyming objects. For a list of these, see the section on rhyming in Chapter 10. Place the objects on the table one at a time, naming each one. After they are all displayed, let children take turns picking up pairs of rhyming objects. Have the group recite the rhyming pair as it is picked up. After all the objects have been collected, ask each child, "What rhymes with ___?" (name one of the objects). The child should respond by naming the other object he is holding. Then have each child pass his objects to the child to his left or right, and ask the question again.

Rhyming Card Game. Use a set of pictured words that contain rhyming pairs. Mix the cards up and lay them out faceup. Say the names of two of the cards, and have the children put thumbs-up if they rhyme and thumbs-down if they don't rhyme. Then let children take turns picking up a card and finding its matching rhyming card.

Rhyming Read-Alouds. Read any of the following books, and stop to point out the pairs of rhyming words that are heard:

> *There's a Wocket in My Pocket!* by Dr. Seuss
> *One Fish, Two Fish, Red Fish, Blue Fish* by Dr. Seuss
> *Hop on Pop* by Dr. Seuss
> *Moose on the Loose* by Carol Partridge Ochs
> *Read-aloud Rhymes for the Very Young* by Jack Prelutsky

Breaking Words Into Syllables

Collect a bag of toy animals, foods, or other objects that have a variety of syllables. As each object is taken out of the bag, children are guided to clap, or drum, or count on their fingers the number of syllables in the object's name. This same activity can be done with the months of the year, children's names, or objects spotted around the room. Pennies can be used to make the game more interesting. Have children take turns dropping a penny into a jar for each part of the word. The same activity can be done using a deck of cards containing pictures of objects with varying numbers of syllables. Each child draws a card from the pile, claps the number of syllables, and takes that number of pennies or other tokens. This can be a fun activity during snack time. Tokens can be small snack foods, such as Goldfish or soup crackers.

Syllable and Sound Blending

As you say the syllables or sounds in some simple words, slide pennies, plastic chips, or other tokens one at a time toward the child, making sure they are going in left-to-right progression for the child. Start with two-syllable words, such as "cupcake." Then try some three- or four-syllable words. If syllable blending is successful, try having the child blend individual sounds. For example, produce each of the sounds $m \ldots a \ldots t$, sliding out a token and pausing after each sound, and ask the child to figure out the word you said. If the child gets the word correct, he can put the pennies or poker chips into a cup or container.

Alphabet Letter Names and Sounds

Alphabet Song. Using a wall chart of the alphabet letters, have the children sing the song as each letter is touched.

Trail of Letters. Using either capital or lowercase letters (start with capitals as these are generally acquired first and are easier to recognize), create a trail across the floor from *A* to *Z*. Have children take turns walking the trail as they say or sing the alphabet.

Letter Find. Supply each player with a strip of paper displaying the alphabet letters. Place letter tiles facedown on the table. As you name a letter, have players take turns picking up and placing the corresponding letter tile on the letter named.

Name Game. Each person has a strip with his or her name in uppercase letters. Players take turns drawing letter tiles. If the letter is in their name, it is placed on their name card. Keep playing until all the names are completed.

Alphabet Soup 1. Put a set of letter tiles in a bowl with a spoon. Each person has a card with a short word, such as "cat" or "dog." Have players take turns drawing letter tiles until the words are completed.

Alphabet Soup 2. Each player has an empty bowl. Players take turns picking up letter tiles that have been placed facedown on a table. If the player can name the letter and/or letter sound, the tile can go in his bowl.

Alphabet Soup 3. Put a set of alphabet letter tiles in a bowl and give each player a small empty bowl and spoon. Players take turns retrieving letter tiles with their spoons. In order to keep a letter and place it in his own bowl, the child must name the letter and the sound it makes, then think of a word that begins with that sound.

Beginning Sounds. Create or purchase a set of cards showing pictures of objects that begin with various letter sounds. If possible, have four cards for each beginning consonant; for example, for the letter *b,* the pictures can be of a "bear," "boot," "boat," or "ball". Present the child with three cards—for example, cards showing a man, a mop, and a car—and have him pick the two words that begin with the same sound. Ask, "Which two start with the same sound?" If this is difficult for the child, you might try calling attention to the beginning sound by pointing to your mouth as you say the beginning sound of the word. Instruct the child to watch your mouth as you say the words.

- **Beginning Sound Card Search.** Place a portion of the deck of beginning-sound cards faceup on the table. Let children take turns identifying two that begin with the same sound. When a child finds a match, he gets to pick up the cards.
- **Beginning Sound Go Fish.** This is a more difficult game, suitable for five- and six-year-olds. Deal four cards to each player. Each player asks for a specific beginning sound: "Do you have something that begins with *b,* like bear?"

(See Also Top Ten Activities for Five- to Six-Year-Olds in Chapter 5.)

Activities to Promote Peer Interaction

Snack Table for Two. Set up a small table with two chairs in a quiet corner of the classroom. Create a snack that children can serve themselves, by providing a small pitcher of juice or milk, a choice of dry snacks, and some plates, cups, and napkins. Leave pictorial instructions displayed so the children know what to do. Children can invite a peer to share the snack with them. The children can assist each other in deciding who is going next. This arrangement usually promotes one-on-one conversation between the two children. Less verbal or shy children will need some prompting in selecting someone to invite, learning what to say, and so forth. The teacher should demonstrate the procedure in front of the class, inviting a fellow teacher, for example, to have a snack and narrate the snack procedure.

Barrier Games. Two children sit facing each other separated by a barrier—a game board, for example, turned on its side and folded slightly so it stands up. Each child is given an identical set of one of the following: blocks of various shapes and colors, Colorforms, tangrams, colored shapes, pictures of people or scenes, or large colored beads and a string. One child is designated the speaker; the other, the listener. The speaker creates a design or pattern on his side of the barrier, giving directions to the listener for each step. The listener must follow each direction, asking for repetition or clarification if necessary. Here is a sample of dialogue from this activity:

> CHILD 1: Take a large red block and put it down.
> CHILD 2: Okay, what's next?
> CHILD 1: Take a yellow triangle and put it on top.
> CHILD 2: Standing up or lying flat?
> CHILD 1 Standing up.
> CHILD 2: Okay.
> CHILD 1: Now take a long blue one and put it on top of the red one and next
>   to the yellow triangle.
> CHILD 2: Standing up?
> CHILD 1: Yes.

The goal is to end up with an identical design or pattern. At an appropriate time, the teacher can pick up the barrier to let the children see if the designs match. If they match, praise the speaker for giving good directions and the other child for doing good listening. This activity will require adult supervision and assistance to go smoothly. If this activity is too challenging for some children, it can be modified by having the partners sit side by side and take turns directing each other. Another modification would be to place two easels back to back with identical paint colors, and have one child direct the other to create a similar picture.

A similar commercially available game is Guess Who. Each player has an identical tray of peoples' faces and names that can be flipped up or down. Players take turns asking questions to find out the identity of their partner's person, pictured on a corresponding card selected from a deck.

Howdy Pardner. Have the children pair off and go off in pairs to various corners or spots in the room where they can talk quietly to each other in order to find out one of the following about their partner:

- Favorite food
- Favorite color
- Who is in the partner's family
- Three toys the partner likes to play with
- Other fact

Then gather as a group, and have each child report on what she or he found out.

Other partner activities: Send a pair of children on an errand together or assign a collaborative project, such as creating a tangram design, computer graphic, collage, or painting,

Go Ask Alex. Assign one child to be the official helper of the day. (A special hat can be worn if desired.) Instead of being the teacher's helper, he or she can be designated to help classmates who need assistance. When a child asks for help, the teacher can defer appropriate requests to this child by saying, "Can you go ask Alex? He's the helper today."

Go Fish. Any deck of matching card pairs will do for this fun game. Design your own versions using small pictures depicting actions, or create pairs with features that vary in size or color. For example, there can be cards depicting orange fish with green tails, orange fish with red tails, yellow fish with green tails, and so forth. This will require the child to use more specific language in order to request a card—for example, "Do you have an orange fish with a blue tail?" or "Do you have a small, blue bird?"

Appendix B

Resources

Books and Publications

Beyond Baby Talk by Kenn Apel and Julie J. Masterson (Prima Publishing)
It Takes Two to Talk: A Parent's Guide to Helping Children Communicate by Ayala
    Manolson (Hanen)
Read With Me! by Shari Robertson and Helen Davig (Thinking Publications)
Books Are for Talking, Too! by Jane L. Gebers (Pro-Ed)
Fold a Book by Monica Gustafson (Pro-Ed)
Ladders to Literacy (Brookes Publishing Co.)
*Learning Language and Loving It: A Guide to Promoting Children's Social, Language,
    and Literacy Development* by Elaine Weitzman (Hanen)
*Overcoming Dyslexia: A New and Complete Science-Based Program for Reading
    Problems at Any Level* by Sally Shaywitz (Alfred A. Knopf)
Phonemic Awareness in Young Children by Marilen Jager Adams, Barbara R.
    Fuorman, Ingvar Lundbert, and Terri Beller (Brookes Publishing Co.)
A Child Becomes a Reader by Bonnie B. Armbruster, Fran Lehr, and Jean Osborn
    (available online at *www.nifl.gov/partnership*)
Put Reading First: Helping Your Child Learn to Read by The Partnership for Reading
    (available online at *www.nifl.gov*)

Computer Programs

Little Planet (Houghton Mifflin Co.)
Earobics (Cognitive Concepts)
Sequential Software for Language Intervention and Development (Laureate Learning
    Systems)

Videos

Good Talking with You Series (Educational Productions)

Commercial Companies for Educational Products

Cognitive Concepts   888-328-8199 *www.earobics.com*
Educational Productions   800-950-4949 *www.edpro.com*
Educators Publishing Service   800-225-5750 *www.epsbook.com*
The Hanen Centre   416-921-1073 *www.hanen.org*
Laureate Learning Systems, Inc. 800-655-4755 *www.LaureateLearning.com*
LinguiSystems   800-776-4332 *www.linguisystems.com*
Lakeshore Learning Materials   800-421-5354 *www.lakeshorelearning.com*
Brookes Publishing Company   800-638-3775 *www.brookespublishing.com*
Pro-Ed, Inc.   800-897-3202 *www.proedinc.com*
Super Duper Publications   800-277-8737 *www.superduperinc.com*
Thinking Publications   800-225-4769 *www.thinkingpublications.com*
The Psychological Corporation 800-763-2306 *www.psychorp.com*

Organizations

American Library Association (ALA)
800-545-2433   *www.ala.org*

American Speech-Language-Hearing Association (ASHA)
800-638-8255   *www.asha.org*

The International Dyslexia Association
410-296-0232   *www.interdys.com*

International Reading Association
800-336-READ (336-7323)   *www.reading.org*

International Society for Technology in Education
800-336-5191   *www.iste.org*

National Association for the Education of Young Children (NAEYC)
800-424-2460   *www.naeyc.org*

National Child Care Information Center (NCCIC)
800-616-2242   *www.nccic.org*

National Head Start Association
703-739-0875   *www.nhsa.org*

National Institute for Literacy (NIFL)
202-233-2025   *www.nifll.org*

Public Library Association (A Division of the American Library Association)
800-545-2433   *www.pla.org*

Reading Is Fundamental
877-RIF-READ   *www.rif.org*

Visit a Virtual Library: Web Sites with Online Books for Kids

(Thanks to Judith Kuster who published a larger list of these in the ASHA Leader.)

Internet Public Library *www.ipl.org*
Billy Bears Story Books *www.billybears4kids.com/story/books.htm*
Children's Storybooks Online *www.magickeys.com*
Starfall (Interactive Books) *www.starfall.com*
Clifford the Big Red Dog *http://pbskids.org/clifford/stories/index.html*
Book Pop Virtual Library *www.bookpop.com*
Storyville *www.alfy.com/Storyville*
Li'l Fingers *www.lil-fingers.com*
Planet Esme *www.planetesme.com*

Bibliography

American Academy of Pediatrics. "Media Education." *Pediatrics* 104 (1999): 341-343.

Agin, M. C., L. F. Geng, and M. J. Nicholl. *The Late Talker.* New York: St. Martin's Press, 1999.

Anderson, R. M., M. Miles, and P. A. Matheny. *Communicative Evaluation Chart From Infancy to Five Years.* Cambridge, Mass.: Educators Publishing Service, 1963.

Apel, K., and J. J. Masterson. *Beyond Baby Talk.* Roseville, Calif.: Prima Publishing, 2001.

Applebee, A. N. *The Child's Concept of Story.* Chicago: University of Chicago Press, 1978.

Aram, D., and J. Nation. "Preschool Language Disorders and Subsequent Language and Academic Difficulties." *Journal of Communication Disorders,* 13 (1980): 159-179.

Barone, D. M., and L. M. Morrow, eds. *Literacy and Young Children.* New York: Guilford Press, 2003.

Bishop, D., and K. Mogford. *Language Development in Exceptional Circumstances.* Hove, East Sussex, England: Lawrence Erlbaum Associates, 1993.

Blank, M. *Teaching Learning in the Preschool.* Cambridge, Mass.: Brookline Books, 1988.

Bloom, L., and M. Lahey. *Language Development and Language Disorders.* New York: John Wiley, 1978.

Boehm, A. E. *Boehm 3 Preschool/Boehm Test of Basic Concepts.* The Psychological Corporation, 2001.

Bowman, B., S. Donovan, and S. Burns. eds. *Eager to Learn: Educating Our Preschoolers.* Washington, D.C.: National Academy Press, 2001.

Carson, B. *Gifted Hands: The Ben Carson Story.* Grand Rapids, Mich.: Zondervan, 1990.

Catts, H. W. "The Early Identification of Language-Based Reading Disabilities." *Language, Speech, and Hearing Services in Schools,* 28 (1997): 86-89.

Catts, H. W. *Reading Disabilities: A Developmental Language Perspective.* Needham Heights, Mass.: Allyn & Bacon, 1991.

_____., M. E. Fey, J. B. Tomblin, and X. Zhang. "A Longitudinal Investigation of Reading Outcomes in Children with Language Impairments." *Journal of Speech, Language, and Hearing Research,* 45 (2002): 1142-1157.

Cazden, C. *Classroom Discourse: The Language of Teaching and Learning.* Portsmouth, N.Y.: Heinemann, 1988.

Chermak, G. D., and F. E. Musiek. *Central Auditory Processing Disorders.* San Diego, Calif.: Singular Publishing Group, 1997.

Clements, D. H., and J. Sarama. "Young Children and Technology: What Does the Research Say?" *Young Children,* November 2003.

Codell, E. R. *How to Get Your Child to Love Reading.* Chapel Hill, N. C.: Algonquin Books of Chapel Hill, 2003.

Copeland, R. *Piagetian Activities: A Diagnostic and Developmental Approach.* Eau Claire, Wis.: Thinking Publications, 1988.

Crago, M. "Development of Communicative Competence in Inuit Children: Implications for Speech-Language Pathology." *Journal of Childhood Communication Disorders,* 13 (1990): 73-83.

Cross, T. "Habilitating the Language-Impaired Child: Ideas From Studies of Parent-Child Interaction." *Topics in Language Disorders,* 4 (1984): 1-14.

Davis, D. S. *A Parent's Guide to Middle Ear Infections.* Stanhope, N.J.: Hear You Are, 1994.

Dickson, D. K., and P. Tabors. *Beginning Literacy with Language.* Baltimore, Md.: Paul H. Brooks, 2001.

Dore, J. "Variation in Preschool Children's Conversational Performances." In K. Nelson, ed., *Children's Language Volume 1,* 397-444. New York: Gardner Press, 1978.

Dougherty, D. P. *How To Talk to Your Baby.* Garden City Park, N.Y.: Avery Publishing Group, 1999.

Elkind, D. *The Hurried Child.* Cambridge, Mass.: Perseus Publishing, 2001.

Espinosa, L. M. "High-Quality Preschool: Why We Need It and What It Looks Like." *Preschool Policy Matters* 1 November. Available online at *nieer.org/resources/policybriefs/1.pdf*

Farber, J. G., and M. Goldstein. "Parents Working With Speech-Language Pathologists to Foster Partnerships in Education." *Language, Speech and Hearing Services in Schools,* 29 (1998): 24-34.

Gallagher, A., U. Frith, and M. J. Snowling. "Precursors of Literacy Delay Among Children at Genetic Risk of Dyslexia." *Journal of Child Psychology and Psychiatry,* 41 (2000): 203-213.

Gard, A., L. Gilman, and J. Gorman. *Speech and Language Development Chart.* Austin, Tex.: Pro-Ed, 1993.

Gebers, J. L. *Books Are for Talking, Too!* Tucson, Ariz.: Communication Skill Builders, 1995.

Golinkoff, R. M., and K. Hirsh-Pasek. *How Babies Talk*. New York: Penguin Putnam, 1999.

Good Talking With You: Language Acquisition Through Conversation. Portland, Ore.: Educational Productions.

Gortmaker, L. L., A. Must, and A. M. Sobol. "Television Viewing as a Cause of Increasing Obesity Among Children in the United States 1986-1990." *Archives of Pediatrics and Adolescent Medicine*, 150 (1996): 356-362.

Hart, B., and T. Risley. *Meaningful Differences in the Everyday Experience of Young American Children*. Baltimore, Md.: Paul H. Brooks, 1995.

_____.*The Social World of Children: Learning to Talk*. Baltimore, Md.: Paul H. Brookes, 1999.

Heath, S. B. "What No Bedtime Story Means: Narrative Skills at Home and School." In B. Mayor and A. Pugh., eds., *Language, Communication and Educatio,*. 259-283. N.H.: Croom-Helm, 1987.

Heath, S. M., and J. H. Hogben. "Cost-Effective Prediction of Reading Difficulties." *Journal of Speech, Language, and Hearing Research,* 47 (2004): 751-765.

Hoff-Ginsberg, E. "Why and How Some Mothers Talk More to Their Children Than Other Mothers." Paper presented at the Biennial Meeting of the Society for Research in Child Development, Seattle, Washington, April 18-20, 1991.

Hurley, S. Suggestions for successful play dates, personal communication, 1994.

Ilg, F. L., L. B. Ames, J. Haines, and C. Gillespie. *School Readiness*. New York: Harper & Row, 1978.

Johnson, K., and B. Heinze. *Hickory Dickory Talk: A Family Approach to Infant and Toddler Language Development*. East Moline, Ill.: LinguiSystems, 1990.

Johnston, E. B., B. D. Weinrich, and A. R. Johnson. *A Sourcebook of Pragmatic Activities*. Tucson, Ariz.: Communication Skill Builders, 1984.

Justice, L. M., M. A. Invernizzi, and J. D. Meier. "Designing and Implementing an Early Literacy Screening Protocol: Suggestions for the Speech-Language Pathologist. *Language, Speech, and Hearing Services in Schools,* 33 (2002): 84-101.

Justice, L. M. "Emergent literacy: What Are Developmentally Appropriate Practices for Preschoolers?" Presentation at the annual ASHA convention, Philadelphia, Penn., 2004.

Kamhi, A. G. "Causes and Consequences of Reading Disabilities." In A.Kamhi, and H. Catts, eds., *Reading Disabilities: A Developmental Language Perspective*. Needham Heights, Mass.: Allyn & Bacon, 1991.

U.S. Dept. of Health and Human Services, Office of Human Development Services, Administration for Children, Youth and Families, Head Start Bureau.

Mainstreaming Preschoolers: Children with Speech and Language Impairments. DHHS Publication Number (OHDS) 81-31113.

Manolson, A. *It Takes Two to Talk*. Toronto, Ont.: The Hanen Center, 1992.

———. *You Make the Difference*. Toronto, Ont.: The Hanen Center, 1995.

Maxwell, K. and R. M. Clifford. "Research in Review: School Readiness Assessment." *Young Children,* 59 (2004): 42-46.

McArthur, G. M., J. H. Hogben, V. T. Edwards, S. M. Heath, and E. D. Mengler. "On the 'Specifics' of Specific Reading Disability and Specific Language Impairment." *Journal of Child Psychology and Psychiatry,* 41 (2000): 869-874.

Murphy, K. L., R. DePasquale, and E. McNamara. "Meaningful Connections: Using Technology in Primary Classrooms." *Young Children,* November 2003.

NAEYC. NAEYC Position Statement: Technology and Young Children—Ages Three Through Eight, 1996. Available online at *naeyc.org/resources/ positionstatements/pstech98.htm*.

Nation, K., P. Clare, C. M. Marshall, and M. Durand. "Hidden Language Impairments in Children: Parallels Between Poor Reading Comprehension and Specific Language Impairment?" *Journal of Speech, Language, and Hearing Research,* 47 (2004): 199-211.

Perkins, A. *Hand, Hand, Fingers Thumb*. Bright & Early Books for Beginning Readers, 1969.

Peura, R., and C. J. DeBoer. *Storymaking: Using Predictable Literature to Develop Communication*. Eau Claire, Wis.: Thinking Publications, 2003.

Pike, S. L. *"Mother-Child Discourse: Cultural and Socioeconomic Factors Across Three Situations."* Ph.D. diss. University of Virginia, 1997.

Rice, M. L., and K. A. Wilcox. *Building a Language-Focused Curriculum for the Preschool Classroom*. Vol.1: *A Foundation for Lifelong Communication*. Baltimore, Md.: Paul H. Brooks, 1995.

Scarborough, H. S. "Very Early Language Deficits in Dyslexic Children." *Child Development,* 61 (1990): 1728-1743.

Schwartz, S. *The New Language of Toys*. Bethesda, Md.: Woodbine House, 2004.

Sharp, C. *Now You're Talking: Techniques That Extend Conversations Facilitator's Guide*. Portland, Ore.: Educational Productions, 1987.

Shaywitz, S. *Overcoming Dyslexia*. New York: Alfred A. Knopf, 2003.

Shields, M. K., and R. E. Behrman. "Children and Computer Technology: Analysis and Recommendations." *The Future of Children,* Vol. 10 No. 2, 2000.

Silliman, E. R. "Interactional Competencies in the Instructional Context: The Role of Teaching Discourse in Learning." In G. P. Wallach and K. G. Butler, eds., *Language Learning Disabilities in School-Age Children*, 288-317. Baltimore, Md.: Williams & Wilkins, 1984.

Snow, C. E. "Parent-Child Interaction and the Development of Communicative Ability." In R. Schiefelbusch, ed. *The Development of Communicative Competence,* Volume 5. 1982.

Snow, C. E., M. S. Burns, and P. Griffin, eds. *Preventing Reading Difficulties in Young Children.* Washington, D.C.: National Academy Press, 1998.

Snowling, J. J., D. V. M. Bishop, and S. E. Stothard. "Is Preschool Language Impairment a Risk Factor for Dyslexia in Adolescence?" *Journal of Child Psychology and Psychiatry,* 41 (2000): 587-600.

STILL unacceptable trends in kindergarten entry and placement (National Association of Early Childhood Specialists in State Departments of Education [NAECS/SDE] position statement, endorsed by NAEYC): *www.naeyc.org/resources/position statements/psunacc.pdf*

Stipek, D. "At What Age Should Children Enter Kindergarten? A Question for Policy Makers and Parents." *Social Policy Report,* 16 (2002): 3-17. Available online at *www.srcd.org/sprv17n2.pdf*

Swank, L. K. and H. W. Catts. "Phonological Awareness and Written Word Decoding." *Language, Speech, and Hearing Services in Schools,* 25 (1994): 9-14.

Tannen, D. *You Just Don't Understand.* New York: William Morrow, 1990.

Trelease, J. *Read-Aloud Handbook.* Penguin Publishing, 2001.

Ukrainetz, T. A. "Stickwriting Stories: A Quick and Easy Narrative Notation Strategy." *Language, Speech, and Hearing Services in Schools,* 29 (1998): 197-207.

Van Kleeck, A., R. Gillam, L. Hamilton, and C. McGrath. "The Relationship Between Middle-Class Parents' Book-Sharing Discussion and Their Preschoolers' Abstract Language Development." *Language, Speech, and Hearing Services in Schools,* 29 (1997): 11-19.

Weitzman, E. *Learning Language and Loving It.* Toronto, Ont.: Hanen, 1992.

Westby, C. "Development of Narrative Language Abilities." In G. Wallach and K. Butler, eds., *Language Learning Disabilities in School-Age Children,* 103-127. Baltimore, Md.: Williams & Wilkins, 1984.

Westby, C. "Children's Play: Reflection of Social Competence." *Seminars in Speech and Language,* 9 (1988): 1-14.

Whitehurst, G., F. Falco, C. Lonigan, J. Fischel, B. DeBaryshe, M. Valdez-Menchaza, and M. Caulfield. "Accelerating Language Development Through Picture Book Reading." *Developmental Psychology,* 24 (1988): 552-559.

Zimmerman, I. L., V. G. Steiner, and R. E. Pond. *Preschool Language Scales,* 4th ed. The Psychological Corporation, 2002.

Index